FIRST PETER

A Reformed Study of the Living
and Abiding Word of God

John Dayton

CONTENTS

Preface

Until 1979, while I was a pilot in the Air Force, I lived as you might expect of such a young, single man in his mid-20s. Church, the Bible, and Christianity were not part of my life until then. I planned to leave the Air Force, attend graduate school, and become a theoretical physicist. God had other plans. During my last year in the service, in 1979, I had a sudden and unexpected born-again experience that I hadn't asked for. If someone had told me I would write expository commentaries on the Bible during my latter years, I would have thought they were crazy.

I did go to graduate school and earned my PhD in physics. However, as a new Christian, I was naive and thought all churches are Christian churches that preach from the Bible and proclaim the gospel. It took a few years for reality to sink in and to realize that not all churches honor and glorify the Lord Jesus Christ as they should. I thank the Lord for being led to a Reformed church where the pure word of God is preached. Like most new converts, I harbored the same false notions of what the Christian faith is and found it difficult to accept the tenets of the Reformed faith.

However, the Reformed faith is the faith of the Apostles, who wrote to us about it as taught by Jesus Christ. The divisions between the Reformed faith and the various non-reformed faiths, though they express many doctrines with the same language, lie in the false presupposition they begin with and the theological consequences of them. The only

1

presuppositions of Reformed theology are that God is and that Scripture is the sole authoritative source of truth concerning faith and life. The remainder of Reformed theology is derived exclusively from Scripture. False presuppositions lead people with reasonable minds, godly intentions, and good consciences to misinterpret important Scriptures and develop errant doctrines and divergent theologies.

First Peter: A Reformed Study of the Living and Abiding Word of God, as the title states, follows Reformed theology. In every place, as much as possible, I included Scripture references to establish the truth extracted from Peter's text. While this is a deep delve into Peter's text, it is an easy read for anyone. Concepts of our faith are explored with a wider breadth to establish the fullness of their truth in the context of the Bible with many Scripture proofs. Multiple translations of the Bible were referenced, along with using a Greek interlinear and lexicon to establish the current statements of difficult passages. The heavy lifting, so to speak, was done in the writing of this commentary. It is a valuable resource for anyone digging deeply into 1 Peter and for those leading a study of this epistle.

May the Lord add his blessing to the reading of First Peter.

An Introduction to the Apostle Peter and First Peter

Peter, who was named Simon Bar-Jonah, was born about 1 B.C. He and his brother Andrew were Galilean fishermen who, along with Philip, were born and lived in Bethsaida, a small village north of the Sea of Galilee and east of the Jordan River. Galilee is the northern part of Israel, bordered on the east by the Sea of Galilee and the Jordan River.

Peter is introduced to us in Scripture with the best details found in John's Gospel. Simon's brother Andrew had heard John the Baptist speak and followed Jesus. He alerted Simon that he had seen the Messiah and took Simon to meet Jesus. When they arrived, Jesus said to Simon that he would be called Cephas (John 1:40-42). Cephas is Aramaic for "stone" or "rock." In Greek, it is Petros, which is derived from Peter.

This relates to Peter's calling as a disciple, made more evident by Matthew, who indicates Peter and his brother Andrew were the first of the twelve apostles to be called (Mat 4:18-20).

We are often told that Peter was the first to call Jesus the Christ. That may not be technically correct. Before Peter met Jesus, his brother Andrew called Jesus the Messiah (John 1:41). Shortly after Peter was called, Nathaniel called Jesus "the Son of God, the King of Israel" (John 1:49). Peter put it all together and called Jesus "the Christ, the Son of the Living God" (Matt. 16:16). Andrew identified Jesus by his office or calling, Nathaniel identified Jesus by his person, and Peter put the two together.

We learn of Peter's propensity for making hasty decisions and speaking all too quickly.

- Peter jumps out of the boat to walk on the water but needs to be saved. Matt. 14:28-30

- Peter rebukes Jesus not to go to Jerusalem. Matt. 16:22

- Peter claims that he will never fall away. Matt. 26:33

- Peter initially refuses to let Jesus wash his feet. John 13:8

- Peter draws a sword and cuts off the right ear of the high priest's servant. John 18:10

He is a man of great faith who can proclaim the Gospel.

- Peter speaks for a twelfth apostle to be named. Acts 1:14-22

- Peter's great sermon during Pentecost. Acts 2:14-36.

- Peter's address on Solomon's Portico. Acts 3:12-26

- Peter before the Council. Acts 4:8-12

- Peter before the Council a second time. Acts 5:29-32

- Peter proclaims the Gospel to Cornelius, a Gentile. Acts 10:34-43

- Peter reports to the church. Acts 11:4-17

There are several other essential events in Peter's life of faith.

- Healing a crippled beggar. Acts 3:1-8
- Many healed, many signs and wonders. Acts 5:12-16
- Put in Prison but released by an angel. Acts 5:17-19
- Healed the paralytic Aeneas. Acts 9:32-34
- Resurrects a disciple named Tabitha. Acts 9:39-41
- Peter was arrested by King Herod but released from prison by an angel. Acts 12:1-11
- Jesus foretells how Peter will be put to death. John 21:18-19

Tradition holds that Peter was martyred sometime around 67 A.D. Peter is the only author in the New Testament who includes hypocrisy among other sins he lists. He was once called out for this sin of hypocrisy when he withdrew from eating with Gentiles out of fear of the circumcision party (Gal. 2:11-14).

Peter's Journeys

As recorded in Acts, Peter and John were sent to Samaria to teach the word of God (Acts 8:14). Peter went to Lydda (Acts 9:32), where he healed a paralyzed man named Aeneas. Moving on to Joppa, he resurrected a woman named Tabitha in Acts 9:36. He then went to Caesarea to preach to Cornelius (Acts 10).

Peter was in Antioch of Syria, as Paul described in his epistle to the Galatians. Peter was conducting himself well until men from Jerusalem came to Antioch and taught that Gentiles must be circumcised. This led him to visibly withdraw from the Gentile believers, for which Paul had no hesitation to rebuke Peter for doing so.

In Paul's first letter to the Corinthians, he mentions Peter several times by the name Cephas. The tone of these passages is that the Corinthians know who Cephas is by more than reputation. This doesn't prove Peter was in Corinth; it only indicates that he might have been. If so, it would place him closer to Rome, but that's a matter of speculation.

Peter is often cited as having written 1 Peter while in Rome. However, there is no reliable evidence that he was ever in Rome. He might have established a church in Rome, but there is no historical reference from before the middle of the second century (see britannica.com). There is no mention in Acts of Peter having journeyed to Rome and no mention of Peter in Paul's epistle to the Romans or Paul's epistles written from Rome. In 1 Peter 5:12, Peter mentions Silvanus as a faithful brother. Silvanus is known for traveling with Paul and was with Paul in Corinth when Paul wrote 1 and 2 Thessalonians, but it is not known if Silvanus was with Paul in Rome. Peter also mentions that Mark sent his greetings in 5:13. We know that Mark was with Paul in Rome at some time (Col. 4:10). Although both apostles mention Mark and Silvanus in their epistles, neither mentions the other. It is equally unclear when 1 Peter was written. Dates range from the early 60s to the early 80s AD. The later dates are suggested by "scholars" who do not ascribe the letter to Peter.

The First Epistle of Peter

Peter's first epistle is written to Jews dispersed across Asia Minor and living as exiles or strangers in a foreign land. The central theme of 1 Peter is that Christians should expect trials and suffering for their faith. But it is their faith that God uses to guard them through their suffering. He explains at length the proper response and attitude of Christians while suffering and relates their suffering to Christ's. He often draws us to the very end of the age when Christ will reappear so that we may contemplate the glory of Christ, the righteous judgment of the wicked, and the end of suffering. They are encouragements to our hope and for strengthening our faith.

There are wonderful discoveries ahead as we study 1 Peter. In Chapter 1, we come upon the grace of God that has caused us to be born again. No sooner do we read of that wonderful reality that we are led in our mind's eye to an imperishable, undefiled, and unfading inheritance now being kept in heaven and guarded for us. In Chapter 2, the splendor of the church is presented. It is a panoramic portrayal of who and what the saints have become—living stones, a chosen race, a royal priesthood, a holy nation that is being built into a spiritual house. Chapters 3 and 4 are filled with exhortations concerning relationships and continuing instruction on suffering as a faithful Christian. Chapter 5 considers the role of shepherds and overseers in the church and how they are to lead and be respected.

Throughout the epistle, Peter calls Christians to be sober-minded, to remain focused on Christ, and to remain faithful because the God of all grace is faithful, and he has called you to a living hope through the resurrection of Jesus Christ and the glory that will be revealed at the proper time.

Chapter 1 – God's Eternal Plan, The Covenant of Grace

Introduction

We immediately encounter Peter's compressed theology as we begin his first epistle. The first two verses contain only his greeting but express his office and authority as an apostle, an identification of his immediate audience, present the doctrine of election, the sanctifying work of the Holy Spirit, Christ's mediation of the saints, the sprinkling of his blood, and an appeal for saints to be blessed with grace and peace superabundantly. It will take us many pages to work through the content of these two verses.

Following his greeting, Peter sets our minds on the Father's most wonderful mercy and power, poured out on behalf of the saints. The theology of verses 3 through 5 is timeless. It spans all of time, from eternity in the past when the Father chose the saints for glory to eternity to come when they are assembled in glory as the perfected church. All the while, the Father is guarding the saints through faith. These verses encapsulate the theology of Christian faith, expressing a theology that is unmistakenly monergistic, by Christ alone, by grace alone, through faith alone, according to the will of the Father.

The flow of content proceeds naturally. Having established how we came to be saints and the glory that awaits us, Peter addresses his readers' present state of affairs, being pastoral in his approach. He addresses believers struggling with grievous trials and difficulties and endeavors to equip them with the spiritual tools to endure and be faithful witnesses of the one true faith. For further encouragement and strengthening, Peter draws our attention to the prophets of old to confirm the faith that his readers profess, which is what the prophets spoke and wrote about regarding the person of Christ.

Having explained the foundation of our hope and the testimony of the prophets, Peter calls the saints to live lives of obedience, expecting the grace that will be revealed when Christ appears. This is followed by a gentle, pastoral nudge by way of reminding the saints of God's impartial judgment and that they should never forget they were ransomed from their former lives by the precious blood of Christ.

Having brought our thoughts to Christ, Peter expresses Jesus Christ's preeminence over creation and establishes that it is only through Jesus Christ we can come to God and have hope.

1:1-2 Greeting

The phrases of verses 1 and 2 are a simple list of things that have been done or are being done to and for the elect by the Father, the Spirit, and the Son. Their meanings are interwoven and inseparable. The apostle is presenting a unified reality. Peter informs us here that the Father elects, the Son propitiates through the blood of his incarnation, and the Spirit applies grace to us according to the will of the Father.

1 Peter 1:1

Peter the Apostle

Peter begins by identifying himself as the writer of this epistle and his position within the church. He wants the readers to know him through this identity. He is an apostle of Jesus Christ; as such, he has authority directly from Christ to encourage, instruct, exhort, and discipline the church.

The elect

The letter is being sent to believers living in the listed Roman provinces of Asia Minor. They are identified as "exiles of the Dispersion" and considered Jewish converts. Diaspora, translated here as dispersion, refers to Jewish communities living among Gentiles. Their exile may be questioned since it comes from a Greek word for residing in a strange country, translated as strangers in NASB and KJV and as sojourners in other Bibles. In 66 A.D., Judea began a revolt against Rome. The Roman general Titus put Jerusalem under siege and destroyed Jerusalem and the Second Temple in 70 A.D. Jewish families had been in Asia Minor long before the Judean War of 66 A.D., so their presence was not a new development. Many might have settled there after returning from Babylonian captivity, fleeing persecution in Israel, or the Judean War. As we delve into 1 Peter, we find they are not foreigners to suffering and persecution.

Whether Peter is writing to exiles, strangers, or sojourners, he is writing to people he identifies among the elect of God. This is typical of an apostolic greeting. He is not conferring or confirming their election. He is using it as a charitable expression of encouragement and hope. It behooves us to pause momentarily to consider the structure of these initial phrases. Peter begins by identifying that his authority comes from Christ and immediately applies it to his audience to encourage them by referring to them as the elect. There is no doubt that he means the elect of God.

1 Peter 1:2

The foreknowledge of God

This verse needs to be put into the larger context of Scripture, from which we deduce what is known as the covenant of redemption. This was the covenant struck by the three Persons of God before creation. Within this covenant, the Father chose or elected who would be redeemed and planned their redemption. The Son accepted the assignment as Redeemer and agreed to be sent to redeem the elect. The Holy Spirit agreed to apply the work and benefits of Christ to the elect according to the will of the Father. Ephesians 1:2-6 is a beautiful account of this covenant. Paul explains that the Father chose and predestined the elect. This was done in love according to his undisclosed decretive will that the elect would be made blameless and holy by his Son to become adopted sons. Election and predestination are by his grace alone, for which he will be praised. Here, we find the parts of the Father and Son in the covenant of redemption. The part of the Holy Spirit may be deduced.

It is an integral part of the covenant of redemption that the Father assigns a kingdom to the Son (Luke 22:28-30). Jesus explained that the Father gave the Son authority over all flesh and the authority to give eternal life to those the Father had given him (John 17:1-5). The charge he received from the Father was to lay down his life and take it up again with the authority to freely do so of his own accord (John 10:17-18).

The covenant of grace is the working out in time and history of the covenant of redemption. The charge given to the Son by the Father included the entire ministry of the office of Christ as head of the church (Acts 10:41). All things done by Christ were appointed to him by the Father. The office of Christ is an expansive office that was assigned and agreed upon before creation. It includes the humiliation of becoming man, living under the law, the imputation of the guilt of sin, a sacrificial death by being nailed to a cross, mediation, intercession, his reappearing in glory, and being the judge of the living and the dead.

The Holy Spirit's part in the covenant of grace was agreed upon in the covenant of redemption. In Christ, we were sealed by the promised Holy Spirit (Joel 2:28), who is the guarantee of our inheritance (Eph. 1:13-14). Indeed, we see the work of the Holy Spirit as the application of the covenant of grace. Still, the duties of the Holy Spirit, the work he was to do, and his role in the covenant of grace were assigned and agreed upon within the covenant of redemption. As the covenant of grace is the execution of an unfolding consequence of the covenant of redemption, Peter writes that grace and peace will be multiplied to the saints according to how it was ordained and predestined.

We encounter statements of God's foreknowledge in several verses: Acts 2:23; Romans 8:29, 11:2; and 1 Peter 1:2, 20. How we explain God's foreknowledge has a bearing on our theology. Our explanation should be based on and rooted in Scripture. Otherwise, our theology will deviate from the truth. Many Christians explain God's foreknowledge as his peering through the corridors of time to learn about people and events. However, is that belief and its resulting theology based on Scripture alone, or is it mixed with conjecture and presuppositions?

As we continue through 1 Peter, we will see how Scripture opposes such an explanation of the Father's foreknowledge and the theology it generates. Beginning with 1 Peter 1:2, Peter addresses his epistle to the elect and explains they were elected according to the foreknowledge of the Father. The Father's foreknowledge and the sanctifying work of the Holy Spirit result in the elects' obedience to Jesus Christ, not some action they took or the choice they made. There are four things the verse does not allow us to separate: the Father's foreknowledge, the sanctifying work of the Holy Spirit, obedience to Jesus Christ, and election.

The verse also presents a cause-and-effect relation. The Father's foreknowledge is causative, while election and obedience are the effect. In between is the sanctifying work of the Holy Spirit, effectuating the Father's intended outcome

(Rom. 8:27; Heb. 2:4). Scripture informs us that the Holy Spirit is the Spirit of grace, not the spirit of merit (Heb. 10:29). As many Christians do, if we say that God looks through time and sees people choosing to follow Christ as a precondition for election, we have inverted cause and effect and perceive God's attributes of omniscience and sovereignty as inferior to what they truly are. The resulting theology bears on the gospel, all but rendering it graceless if election begins with and salvation depends on the merits of human choice and not purely on the will and grace of God (Rom. 9:11, 11:6; Eph. 2:8). God's foreknowledge and associated issues will be discussed further as we proceed through the epistle.

Sanctification of the Spirit

When you were *in school*, the word "in" refers to you, specifically where you were. When you were or are *in your mother's heart*, the word "in" refers to the state or condition of your mother's heart. In verse 2, the phrase *in the sanctification of the Spirit*, the word "in" refers to the Spirit. You were the object of the Spirit's sanctifying work, as it were, in the heart of the Spirit to sanctify you. This exactly parallels what preceded the foreknowledge of God the Father. The Father is the ***originating cause*** of grace and salvation due to his love, and the Spirit is the ***efficient cause***. There are other places where this construction is employed:

Eph. 1:7- In him [Jesus Christ] we have redemption

Rom. 3:24- The redemption that is in Christ Jesus

Rom. 8:1- there is now no condemnation for those who are in Christ Jesus.

We can say that it is "in Christ Jesus" to redeem the elect and "in Christ Jesus" that there shall be no condemnation of the same, just as it is right to say election is in the Father.

In comparison, "*in the sanctification of the Spirit,*" as expressed in the ESV, and rendered "*through sanctification of the Spirit*" in KJV, and as "*by the sanctifying work of the Spirit*" in NASB. Neither KJV nor NASB on this point are entirely appropriate because they merely render the calling and perfection of the saints as after or consequential to the Father's calling and sanctifying work of the Holy Spirit. Though not incorrect, they miss the deeper meaning that it is essentially in the Father to call the saints and in the Holy Spirit to sanctify them. The Father's foreknowledge wasn't through or by the Holy Spirit. The Father's foreknowledge is primary, originating, and unconditional except for his own will.

This work of sanctification is the process by which holiness and righteousness are imparted to the believer. During this life, this process continues but is only completed or perfected once the believer is raised to glory. As such, this is called **progressive sanctification.** However, at the beginning of this work of the Holy Spirit, the Holy Spirit does what is called an act. This act occurs once and is completed by the Holy Spirit when the individual responds to the grace of regeneration with faith (Rom. 5:1). The Spirit imputes Christ's righteousness, which is external to the believer.

Then, the believer is pronounced legally, or forensically, righteous before God, the Father. This act of justification is also known as *definitive sanctification*. The sanctification Peter is attributing to the Spirit here is both definitive and progressive, for there is not one without the other.

All three Persons of the Trinity are involved in some way in all aspects of the elect's salvation. We regard sanctification as the work of the Holy Spirit, but the Father and the Son are involved. The works of washing, justifying, and sanctifying are done by the Holy Spirit of God in the name of Jesus Christ (1 Cor. 6:11). What we take away from this is that it is all according to the will of the Father and applied by the Spirit based on the merits of the Son.

There is an additional purpose of Peter here, which is to bring our minds to that evidence that testifies that we are indeed foreknown by God, for had we not been foreknown by the Father, we would not now be sanctified by the Holy Spirit.

Obedience to Jesus Christ

However, Peter adds, *"for obedience to Jesus Christ"* (ESV) so that no man might deceive himself by having a false sense of spirituality and practicing vain religion. Obedience to Jesus Christ is impossible without first being chosen by the Father and subsequently sanctified by the Spirit. No man should rest on the assumption that he is among the saints chosen by God without evidence of personal sanctification and obedience to Jesus Christ. Therefore, we may take obedience to mean conforming our will to that of Jesus Christ by surrendering ourselves to the transforming power and grace of the Spirit. Doing this can "*confirm your calling and election*" (2 Pet. 1:10 ESV). Obedience to the words of Jesus Christ is likened to having a well-built house (Luke 4:47-49). The one who rejects Jesus' words and does not keep them remains in darkness and is judged by Jesus' words on the last day (John 12:46-48).

The first mark of a recipient of regenerating grace is a living faith in the Lord Jesus Christ. Such faith marks the beginning of obedience. Improved, continued, and sustained obedience is possible by the sanctifying work of the Spirit and the grace he ministers to us. Peter refers to this obedience, which we have grown into by the Spirit following our rebirth. As we study obedience, we find that it is not only a matter of refraining from evil but, just as importantly, doing good works as doers of the Lord's words.

Sprinkling with his blood

Peter insists that anyone who reads this epistle may know whether or not they are truly among the elect. They must be among those whom God foreknew. This is a statement of doctrine and a condition about which no man may know without evidence. However, the evidence, if it exists, is in the form of three things, as stated by Peter. As noted above, the first of these pieces of evidence is sanctification. The next is obedience to Jesus Christ. Being sprinkled with Christ's blood is the third. A man may deceive himself to be spiritual and a follower of Christ, but unless the blood of Christ sprinkles him, he has no part among the elect.

In the Old Testament Church, the blood of the sacrifice was sprinkled on the various utensils of the temple, the veil, the Mercy Seat, people, and other things (Exod. 29:21). This signified three things: 1- that a blood sacrifice had been made, 2- that it was applied, and 3- that what was sprinkled was then considered holy or fit for sacred use.

In the case of a believer, the shed blood of Christ pays a ransom for sin and propitiates God's wrath, but it has to be applied. The reality of this application is metaphorically addressed as sprinkling and harkens back to Old Testament ceremonies. However, when the Father looks upon a believer, he sees the shed blood of Christ, and there is peace between the believer and the Father. We cannot understand God's absolute, immutable holiness and utter difference from us, for which he has to see the blood of Christ upon his children. But we may embrace the fact that the blood of Christ is most precious to us. Thus, we may consider Peter's opening more than a greeting. It affirms God's covenant with his people, and only his people, and addresses God in three persons.

Grace and peace

The initial grace of regeneration and the onset of peace with the Father are not Peter's topics. He is making the invocation that God will bless, in manifold ways, those who study this letter by strengthening their faith, increasing their knowledge of Christ, encouragement through suffering, and godly living resulting from the sanctifying grace of the Holy Spirit. The apostles did not need to write letters to make a name for themselves. They wrote letters to edify the church, encourage believers, and warn against evil in many forms, including false teachers. Their writings were and continue to be a means of grace to the elect of God. What the New Testament teaches about grace is summarized in the following:

1. Grace is from God and is a product of his mercy (1 Pet. 5:10; 1 Tim. 1:2; 2 Tim. 1:2; Heb. 4:16).

2. Grace is effectual (irresistible) for accomplishing its intended purpose (Eph. 2:5, 8, 3:7; Heb. 13:9; 2 Cor. 12:9).

3. Grace is neither earned nor merited; grace is not a reward (Rom. 11:6; 2 Tim. 1:9).

4. Grace produces regeneration, faith, justification, sanctification, spiritual gifts, eternal life, and glory (Acts. 20:32; Rom. 1:5, 3:4, 4:16, 5:17, 21, 12:6; Eph. 2:8; Titus 3:7; 1 Pet. 3:7, 5:10).

5. Grace is intended for and applied to particular people whom God has called in Jesus (Rom. 11:5; Gal. 1:6; 2 Tim. 1:9; 1 Pet. 5:10).

6. There are means of grace: defending the faith, the teaching of the apostles, the work of the Holy Spirit, and humility.

7. Anything else is not the grace of God (1 Pet. 5:10).

1:3-5 Born Again to a Living Hope Part 1 "The Power of God"

Following this brief introduction to God's eternal plan, Peter presents glimpses of God's mercy, power, and glory and how his eternal plan has already transformed our lives with a living hope.

1 Peter 1:3

Knowing the Father

Of course, the only God Peter refers to is the one true and living God of Abraham, Isaac, and Jacob. But since time has moved beyond their days and the mystery of Christ has been revealed, the only acceptable way to know God today, as he has revealed himself to us, is to know Jesus Christ as Lord. It is imperative to understand that there is no other way to know God than through Jesus Christ. According to Jesus' words recorded in Matthew 11:27, it is only possible to know the Father if Jesus chooses to reveal him. This is wonderfully clear in the Greek interlinear text of John 1:18: "*God no one has seen ever yet [the] only begotten God the [one] being in the bosom of the Father he has made [him] known*" (Ref. biblehub.com).

The begotten God is the Son who is in the bosom of the Father. Though the Father cannot be seen, the Son makes him known through his incarnation as Jesus. We may conclude that the Father cannot be known unless the Son makes him known. Jesus repeats this many times, linking himself with the knowledge of the Father (John 8:19, 14:9; 1 John 2:23). Not only does Christ make the Father known, but a person must also be drawn to Christ before they can know the Father. This is an important point, "no one knows the Father," the very words of Christ. Only Christ knows the Father and whoever he reveals him to. John 14:6 is the summation of this issue of knowing the Father. After Jesus told the apostles that he was going to prepare a place for them, Thomas asked to know the way to where Jesus was going. Jesus replied, *"I am the way, and the truth, and the life. No one comes to the Father except through me"* (John 14:6 ESV).

A person can believe God exists, and they can be devout in the practice of their religion, but unless they have a living and trusting faith in Jesus Christ, they do not know the Father. John Calvin comments on John 14:6, "Wherefore all theology, when separated from Christ, is not only vain and confused but is also mad, deceitful, and spurious; for though the philosophers sometimes utter excellent sayings, yet they have nothing but what is short-lived, and even mixed up with wicked and erroneous sentiments." Commenting on 1 Peter 1:3, Calvin wrote, "Hence they who form their ideas of God in his naked majesty apart from Christ, have an idol instead of the true God, as is the case with the Jews and the Turks."

This is an essential and pivotal issue because of all the world's religions and cults; Christianity is unique in the following respects. Any founder, prophet, or apostle of any other religion, cult, or belief, as important as they may have been to that belief system, was unessential. If there had been no Joseph Smith, Charles Russell, or some other individual, it is not inconceivable that the religions they founded could have been established by someone else. As central as Abraham was to the ratification of the covenant of grace, we must concede that Abraham was not essential to it. But if Christ was removed, there would then be no Christianity, and there would be no way to know God, no redemption, and no salvation.

Blessed be the God and Father

Blessed, or holy, is God the Father, an expression of the state in which God exists. But here, Peter assigns the Father to Jesus Christ as his God and Father and assigns Jesus Christ to us as our Lord. This relationship is expressed more clearly as the verse continues. First, we encounter the Father's great mercy. Mercy itself is the withholding of a just and due penalty, leniency. What follows is according to this great mercy of the Father, but what follows lies beyond mercy, for it is far more than just withholding a due penalty; it is undeserved kindness and benefit; it is grace. Again, we are led to the Father as the originating cause of all we have in Christ.

According to his great mercy, the Father has caused us to be born again. As the Father is the originating cause, we are given glimpses into how or why he is the cause of our salvation. In love, he chose whom to save (Eph. 1:4), and foreknowledge was a part of this election (Rom. 8:29). The mercy Peter refers to in verse 3 is associated with the Father's love and foreknowledge. Romans 8:29 picks it up from there and gets into the predestination of the elect, a different matter. However, predestination is not so different that it does not align with verse 3. From God's love and mercy, he causes the elect to be born again. Into whose image are they born again? It is the beginning of being conformed to the image of his Son, Christ, which is what the elect have been predestined to as adopted sons of God (Eph. 1:5). God's mercy and love are the impetus for our election. We have learned something significant about God. God is merciful. And because he is merciful, we too are to be merciful (Matt. 5:7; Luke 6:36).

The circle is complete. The Father abides in a state of blessedness. It is at that point that Peter begins verse 3. From his blessedness, the Father is merciful to particular people, the elect. Having been born again, they are being conformed to the image of his Son so that they can be merciful and blessed as he is.

Let us not overlook the meaning of "born again." The Greek here translates, "having begotten us again." Who has begotten us? It is the Father. The Father has a genuine intimacy with us that is easily obscured by the phrase "born again." As we have seen, being born again is the very first part of having been predestined by the Father.

Connection with verses 1 and 2: Some connections can be made now. What Peter stated in verses 1 and 2 concerning election, foreknowledge, and sanctification is being restated here concerning mercy and being born again. These are parallel concepts of one reality. The Father's mercy in verse 3 is exclusively upon the elect, for it is only the elect who are born again, and as we will see, it is only those born again who are sanctified.

The resurrection and a living hope

Peter states that we are born to new hope, a living hope or a hope of life. We were, by nature, children of wrath (Eph. 2:3), meaning that all we deserve is the eternal wrath of God. In such a state, our only hope was a false hope of a delusion. But for the elect, God's mercy intervened, and a new hope was given to us, a hope for life itself, having begotten us again to a new life. This is why Paul calls God *the God of Hope* (Rom. 15:13).

But what may be the grounds of this new hope of life? The elect are born again through the resurrection of Jesus Christ from the dead, according to verse 3. That is key. Although the Father causes our new birth, his means are through Christ's resurrection. It is an otherwise impossible resurrection since it is from the dead and thus requires the extraordinary power of God (2 Pet. 1:3). In the same manner, the begetting again of the elect is just as impossible unless it is done by the same power which raised Christ from the dead. Imagine, yes, try to comprehend this single vital truth that the power of God that raised Jesus Christ from the dead, from the grave, is the same power by which God has begotten you again to a new life and a living hope (1 Cor. 6:14; Col. 2:12).

Peter already alluded to Jesus' death in verse 2 when he wrote of the sprinkling of his blood. This draws our attention to Christ's sacrificial death and atoning blood, both for the expiation of sin and the propitiation of God's wrath. So, the resurrection Peter writes of in verse 3 is, in all respects, that of a dead body.

1 Peter 1:4

An imperishable inheritance

Peter continues to draw our minds to what it means to be born again. As he previously wrote, it is to a living hope, but he now writes that it is to an inheritance of an amazing kind. Nothing in this world lasts forever. Our bodies wear out. Even the stars above have their demise in time. All things run down. All things stop and fade away. It is written into the laws of nature that paint peels and stone walls crumble. But the inheritance of the elect is not of this world. It is in heaven and is imperishable, undefiled, and unfading. This inheritance has extraordinary qualities beyond our present ability to comprehend them. But our inheritance is not just in heaven; it is *kept* in heaven, implying that it is secure, protected, and maintained. Furthermore, this inheritance is not just kept in heaven; it is kept in heaven for *us*, the elect. Whether the apostle writes about being born again to a living hope or being called and enlightened, there is a glorious inheritance that is imperishable, undefiled, and unfading for all the saints (Eph. 1:18).

1 Peter 1:5

The power of God

As we go on to verse 5, Peter changes our focus from this extraordinary inheritance to the power of God, which is guarding us. This draws our minds to the reality of this life that unless God were to guard the elect, our hope would be in vain. The defilements of this world extract their toll, and as all things perish according to the nature of this world, we would also perish apart from God. The psalmist understood this and pleaded to God to be guarded and delivered (Ps. 25:20). This guardianship of God extends to our hearts and minds in Christ (Phil. 4:7).

Peter brings us to the concept of faith. We can analyze faith, any faith, as it abides in the mind and manifests itself in various behaviors, and we find that all faith shares some degree of commonality. Except for the saving faith in Christ, the only difference between different belief systems lies in the distinct tenets of each, which is to say that the raw human exercise of faith in Buddha is the same as the raw human exercise of faith in Christ. The true and salvific Christian faith is unique in the following aspects:

Rom. 12:3- It is not the product of the natural mind, nor can it be,

Eph. 2:8- It results from the gift of God's grace,

1 Pet. 1:5- It rests in the power of God,

Heb. 11:6- It is necessary to please God,

Rom 3:28- It is the instrumental cause of justification,

Rom. 1:17- It is what the righteous live by,

1 John 5:4- It is the victory that has overcome the world,

1 Pet. 1:9- It leads to salvation, and

Jas. 2:1- The unique object of the Christian faith is the Lord Jesus Christ.

There are things about the Christian faith, according to Scripture, that are external to the individual but are integral to the Christian faith and that lie beyond raw human ability. Without God's grace and sustaining power, there is no Christian faith. Without Christian faith, there is no justification, no human righteousness, no way to please God, no victory, and no salvation. Without the unique person of Jesus Christ, there is no church, no Christianity, and no hope.

Salvation is ready

As we continue with verse five, we find that the verse is typical of Peter's propensity to cram an extensive amount of theology into a few words. He writes that it is by God's power that people are guarded for salvation. It follows that these people have been born again and are faithful, which divides humankind into two camps. Those being saved and those not being saved.

But Peter has things to tell us about this salvation. First, this salvation is ready. This indicates that all matters and actions on which salvation depends have been performed, resolved, completed, and secured. There is nothing more that remains to be done or accomplished to save God's chosen people. Salvation is just as ready for the yet-to-be-born again as it is for those already born again. But if he writes that salvation is ready, does he imply that we are not yet saved? Indeed not. The saints have been saved, but their salvation, as the sons of God, has yet to be revealed to the world and a groaning creation. Peter is drawing us to the reality that we must wait patiently for our inheritance, though it is kept in heaven for us. He encourages us by informing us that all things needful to be saved and all things about it have been accomplished, for our salvation is now ready to be revealed.

As prepared as it is, we must wait for the Lord's coming. Consider the prodigal son who wanted his inheritance now and could not wait. He left his father and squandered his inheritance in sin. Our Father in Heaven holds our inheritance for us until we are ready and fit to receive it as his sons. That will happen when the entire assembly of saints has been sanctified, in both soul and body, into the very likeness of Christ when the unified church is revealed in the Glory of the Son (Rom. 8:22-23). Peter is encouraging us to wait faithfully and patiently for all that we hope for in Christ with assuredness that the things we hope for are ready and kept in heaven for us, even now.

Treasures we currently possess: Building up to this point of encouragement, Peter has already informed us of a great many treasures of which we have already taken possession. We are the objects of the Father's foreknowledge, mercy, and grace by which he has caused us to be born again, have faith, be sanctified, be granted a living hope, and know him through Jesus Christ, a treasure in itself and guarded by his power. How pitiful we are that, after receiving such treasures, the Father still sees our need to be further encouraged. That being so, we are also encouraged by each

other. So let us encourage one another in the Lord to the end
that we build each other up in faith, hope, and charity.

1:6-9 Born Again to a Living Hope Part 2 "Faith Tested by Trials"

Here, we are first instructed about grievous trials and
their necessity. Peter moves in and out of this theme several
times in the epistle. His focus here is to ground us in our faith
and the joy of our salvation so that these trials do not
overcome us.

1 Peter 1:6

In this, you rejoice

God's mercy and call are the grounds and impetus for our
rejoicing. Peter's idea is more along the lines of exultation.
Even if trials grieve us, we rejoice. We are reminded that even
though, from our perspective, the "last time" seems a long way
off however, in the scope of things, it is just a little while from
now when compared with eternity.

1 Peter 1:7

Tested genuineness of your faith

At present, encouragement is still offered when we suffer
grievous trials. Peter tells us that if we suffer such trials, they
are necessary. There are things to glean from this. First, the
necessity of trials indicates there are reasons and purposes for
these trials. We cannot comprehend God's eternal and
comprehensive plan, but we know he will be glorified

through Jesus Christ. The elect will be revealed in glory as his sons according to Romans 8:28, in which we find three things that go together: 1- being called by God according to his purpose, 2- loving God, and 3- all things work together for good (Rom. 8:28).

Trials are but for a little while. The purpose, or at least a purpose, of such trials is to test the genuineness of our faith. Is Peter telling us that God will test our faith to prove to himself that it is genuine? Not at all. God is guarding us through these trials through the faith that he has provided (see verse 5) so that these trials establish two things: 1- that the genuineness of our faith may be established to us, and 2- that the power of God has guarded us through these trials. Closely examine what is being tested. According to Peter, it is not us being tested or whether we have faith but that our faith is genuine. Only genuine faith is the instrument through which God guards us or leads us through his plan. We need to keep before our minds that God has an eternal, comprehensive plan for each of us individually and for us collectively, within which some things need to happen to us that are, for a while, grievous and challenge our faith. It is as if God is being tested, for we endure such trials only by his power and steadfast faithfulness.

Thus, Peter can proclaim praise, glory, and honor when the time of trials and grievous things ends when Jesus Christ is revealed. Again, we are led to contemplate the last time and the revealing of our salvation. Praise, honor, and glory unto God, Almighty and merciful, for it is only by his mercy, grace, and power that we arrive there and then as adopted sons.

There is an aspect in verse 7 that we must consider. Creation was subjected to corruption, but it was not left without hope (Rom. 8:20). That hope is for creation to be set free from its corruption *"into the freedom of the glory of the children of God"* (Rom. 8:20 ESV). So, if our faith is genuine, let us rejoice when tested by fiery trials, knowing the outcome is safeguarded by God's steadfast and enduring love.

Although it is not the point Peter is making here, we may infer that those who do not have genuine faith, false believers, fall away when trials occur. Jesus explained this when explaining the parable of the sower. Falling away is preceded by having no root in oneself or not being grounded. It is triggered by tribulations or persecutions that arise because of the word—meaning the Gospel (Matt. 13:20-21). What prevents falling away is being rooted, built up in Christ, and established in the faith (Col. 2:6-7). The true believer is rooted in Christ, but the non-believer does not have even the slightest strength in himself to withstand trials, *"no root in himself"* (Matt.13:21). Nothing less than the power of God can guard us through trials and establish that our faith is genuine. That is an amazing encouragement.

The revelation of Jesus Christ

We have come to an essential doctrinal issue: the revelation of Jesus Christ. Peter is not referring to the time of his incarnation when he was conceived in Mary's womb. It is a future event spoken of by Jesus many times and written about by the apostles. To delve into this, here is an excerpt from the Westminster Confession of Faith, Chapter 33 Of the Last Judgment, section 2:

> The end of God's appointing this day is for the manifestation of the glory of His mercy, in the eternal salvation of the elect; and of His justice, in the damnation of the reprobate, who are wicked and disobedient. For then shall the righteous go into everlasting life, and receive that fullness of joy and refreshing, which shall come from the presence of the Lord; but the wicked who know not God, and obey not the Gospel of Jesus Christ, shall be cast into eternal torments, and be punished with everlasting destruction from the presence of the Lord, and from the glory of His power (WCF 33:2).

During the earthly ministry of Jesus Christ, he was undertaking his redemptive work to be the sacrificial lamb of God. It was "in" Jesus to do so, as we have explained the meaning and usage of "in." This included being the suffering servant (Isa. 53:1-3) and lamb of God (John 1:29), but there is much more. It's written in John's Gospel account that Jesus is full of grace but also that Jesus Christ is full of truth (John 1:14), a fact whose significance must not be taken lightly. Jesus spoke of his eventual reappearing and the day of judgment several times. We should trust his words and recognize that many significant things will happen when Jesus Christ comes and fully manifests his glory to all people.

The Last Day, the Day of Judgment when Christ appears: The Father has given all judgment to the Son (Acts 17:30-31; John 5:22) who will come in glory with his mighty angels and be seated on his throne (Matt. 25:21). Everyone will appear before the judgment seat of Christ (2 Cor. 5:10) and give an account of every careless word (Matt. 12:36). Those who have rejected Jesus and his word will be judged by his word (John 3:18, 12:48).

The Last Day, the church when Christ appears: According to the will of the Father, on the last day, those who believe in the Son will have eternal life and be raised to be with him (John 6:40, 54). Those who have died in Christ will be raised first, followed by those who are alive. Together, they will be assembled with the Lord in the air (1 Thess. 4:16-17), see him as he is and be like him (1 John 3:2), and will be with the Lord forever (1 Thess. 4:16-17).

The Last Day, creation when Christ appears: Peter rightly refers to the reappearing of Jesus Christ as a revelation, revealing his fullness in a way previously not disclosed. It is called the last day because, at the very least, it is the last day of human life on the old planet Earth. Cataclysmic destruction by fire occurs (2 Pet. 3:12). The first heaven and earth will pass away (Rev. 21:1), and there will be a new heaven and a new earth (1 Pet. 3:13; Rev. 21.1).

The Last Day, when Christ appears: The last day is a day of judgment and damnation of the reprobate and a day of transformation for those in Christ. That day will dawn like any other day with no realization that it is the last day (1

Thess.5:2). No one knows when that day will be except the Father (Matt. 24:36), so therefore, we are to stay awake (do not slumber in your faith) (Matt. 24:42).

Because we do not know when Christ will reappear, it behooves us all to live as though the day is ready, and he is prepared to be revealed even now. Let's review the events of the last day.

1. The resurrection of Christ signifies that God has fixed the day of judgment.

2. Christ is revealed with his intrinsic glory unveiled.

3. Believers will see him as he is and be transformed into his likeness.

4. Believers will be taken into glory.

5. The Earth and heaven will be consumed by fire, and a new earth and a new heaven will be their replacements.

6. Christ will sit on the white throne judgment seat and judge all people.

7. All the reprobate will be cast into hell.

The Westminster Confession of Faith states that God's glory is revealed in the elect's salvation and the reprobate's judgment and is accomplished by Jesus Christ.

The end of God's appointing this day, is for the manifestation of the glory of his mercy in the eternal salvation of the elect; and of his justice in the damnation of the reprobate, who are wicked and disobedient. (WCF 33.2; cf. Matt. 25:31-34; 2 Thes. 1:9)

More precious than gold

What are the things that are precious to the saints? The blood of Christ, the glory of God, the hope of an eternal kingdom, the promised inheritance, adoption as sons, the complete freedom from sin, and other things are precious to the saints. Peter tells us that our faith is among the items on this list. Gold is a soft metal that is good for shaping and covering things. It is also very chemically inactive and does not rust or corrode. However, even the purest gold refined by fire will eventually perish. Saving faith is more precious than all such gold because, as Peter is leading us to realize, even when all the purest gold dissolves into nothingness, our faith will endure.

1 Peter 1:8

You have not seen him

Peter's method of exhortation is a bit unusual. Instead of exhorting us about what to do or think as Paul does, he graciously commends us as if we are doing and thinking what is right, leading us in the correct direction. Verses 8 and 9 are an example of his style. He affirms that even though we have not seen Christ, we love him. He does not have to defend such a statement, for it is the natural response of anyone spiritually led to Christ. We have not seen Christ and do not see him even now, yet we believe in him, he declares. Peter sees that the outcome of our faith has been obtained: the salvation of our souls. Is he contradicting himself since, in verse 5, he wrote that salvation will be revealed in the last time? There is no contradiction. As he says, salvation will be revealed in the last time as the outcome of our faith that revelation will be to the world and all creation.

Right in line with Peter's declaration of our belief in Christ, whom we have never seen, the writer of Hebrews informs us about faith. Christian faith is not only an assurance of things we hope for, but it is also a conviction of them though we have not seen them (Heb. 11:1). If faith is not directive of one's conduct and behavior, it may not be proper to claim there is conviction.

Inexpressible joy

Once again, Peter, in verse 8, is telling us what we are doing rather than telling us what we should be doing. But he is right because whoever believes and loves Jesus Christ will rejoice. The word in Greek is "exult," which conveys a sense of triumph or overcoming. Let's examine how Peter describes our rejoicing. It is with joy. But that is what rejoicing is; it is a demonstration of joy. Jesus Christ has done for us what we could not do for ourselves by triumphing over sin and death and, in so doing, has redeemed us from the wrath of God. Paul also concludes in Romans 8:37 that our conquest over sin and death is through Jesus Christ. This is why Peter declares that we rejoice or exult with joy.

But that's not all for Peter, who now claims this joy is inexpressible. He means that this joy's full nature, character, and scope lie beyond all human ability to communicate it to another, whether by words or actions. We can only experience it. There is more to this. The joy with which we rejoice is inexpressible to those who do not have the mind of Christ and cannot understand spiritual things that impress them as folly (1 Cor. 2:14). Like Peter, the psalmist expressed this exultation that leads to praise and recognized it involves only certain persons (Ps. 33:1).

He is not yet finished. The drunkard and the fool may carry on with unbounded joy in the depth of their folly, and Peter allows us to have nothing of that in mind, for he stipulates that our joy is filled with glory. Peter is ambiguous here. His usage can mean to render glory or to be filled with glory. To render glory does not mean we have some glory of our own that we can cast upon the Lord to make him more glorious, but as we exult in his glory, we proclaim his glory with joy. It is undoubtedly true that the joy believers experience is glorious because its source lies in the benefits secured by the merits and person of Jesus Christ and the love and mercy of the Father. On the contrary, joy that is not rooted in Christ and does not extol him as Lord is simply mundane happiness. Mundane happiness is the joy found in all alleged spiritual experiences in which the Holy Spirit has no part. Such is void of glory and is readily expressed as it is so often passed from one to another. Try expressing your joy in the Lord to a non-believer; it is inexpressible to him because he cannot spiritually understand it.

1 Peter 1:9

Obtaining the outcome of faith

What follows in verse 9 is essential. This is Peter's main point and what he has been leading us to since verse 3. The saints will persevere by the power of God, working through faith and guarding our faith through trials and suffering. The salvation of our souls leads directly to obtaining the very objects of all we have hoped for by faith. As we have seen, we are saved now, and our inheritance is ready now. Jesus stated this most clearly and definitively in terms of the Father's will, our faith, the gift of eternal life, and his pledge to raise the saints to glory on the last day (John 6:44).

Does verse 9 mean we are saved by faith? Must we first love and believe in Jesus before we can be saved as a precondition? Many Christians think so and interpret John 3:16 as meaning that if you first freely choose to believe in Jesus, you will be saved.

However, John 3:16 is just a factual statement about who has eternal life. Earlier in John 3, Jesus explained the necessity of being born again by the Holy Spirit, not the necessity of pre-existing faith. As we will see in 1 Peter 2, only those born again have eternal life, and only they can believe so as not to spiritually stumble and disobey the gospel (1 Pet. 2:8). Salvation is through faith, not by faith. John 3:16 is easily misunderstood, leading many to think that faith/belief is where salvation begins. It begins with the Father's love, mercy, election, and predestination to eternal life as adopted sons through Jesus Christ (Eph. 1:4-5). The first manifestation of being saved, of which we may be aware, is being born again by the power of God, the same power that raised Jesus from the dead (Col. 2:12). The living hope into which we are born (1 Pet. 1:3) is our faith (Heb. 11:1) by which God guards us (1 Pet. 1:5) through to the last time, the end of days when the sons of God are revealed in glory with Christ (Rom. 8:18-19; 1 Pet. 5:1). Faith is an instrumental factor in salvation, but it is not an originating cause or a meritorious cause.

1:10-12 Born Again to a Living Hope Part 3 "The Mystery of Christ"

The apostle desires that we long for Jesus as did the prophets of old. By such longing, we look to and focus on our salvation and Jesus Christ rather than the concerns of this world.

1 Peter 1:10-12

Concerning this salvation

Peter makes a stunning pronouncement. The prophets of the Old Testament, speaking on behalf of God and recording the very words of the Holy Spirit through inspiration, recorded things they did not fully understand. Yet they understood them well enough to recognize the grace that was coming upon future generations and desired even a glimpse at that treasure (Heb. 11:26) and carefully searched to see it (Matt. 13:17). They understood it well enough to know the Spirit of the One within them was the One who would suffer in person (Acts 3:18) who would in his person be the salvation of his people and reveal the glories of his redemptive administration (Gen. 22:8).

But this was a mystery hidden behind an impenetrable veil that no one could see through. Yet, for the prophets, aspects of this mystery were revealed. They knew they were writing for us and that we would have the meaning of what they wrote opened to our minds as a veil lifted from before our eyes and experience directly what the types in their days only foreshadowed. The prophets wrote of Christ who would suffer; they longed to see and hear what we have seen and heard. Even Moses foresaw Christ (Acts 3:22) as he foresaw the riches of his glory and providence (Heb. 11:26). By this, Peter causes us to pause and consider how dull our longing to know the glory of Christ is. He says of the angels in heaven, even those who dwell in the bliss of heaven, long to look into the things now revealed to us. He understood that the prophets and angels were interested in all things about the Lord Christ, not only who he would be, when he would be, but also when he would return a second time (Joel 2:11), as Peter refers to "*the subsequent glories.*"

In all this, Peter testifies that the glory of Christ is to be desired and valued above all things and directs our attention to the prophets. However, in their day, they did not possess the revelation of Christ as he has been revealed to us, yet they longed to see his day and know of him more deeply. And to the witness of the prophets, Peter adds the testimony of the angels in heaven for what great value it was to them to know the things of Christ for which they longed to look into, though they were not the beneficiaries of his office.

A second look at these verses is necessary. Peter has shown us that the religion of the Hebrews and that of the church are of the same cloth. They are the same. There is and has been one faith under two administrations. He begins by writing, *"Concerning this salvation."* Indeed, he is talking about salvation by Christ through faith, as he has since the beginning. But he immediately turns to the prophets and connects them to Christ and the same faith. They served us by what they wrote. They wrote of Christ who suffered, of his grace and glory. They wrote by the same Holy Spirit that has since empowered men to preach the good news of Jesus Christ and the same Holy Spirit that has been poured out into the modern church (Joel 2:28; Acts 2:2-4).

1:13-16 Called to be Holy Part 1 "Preparation"

Peter is building up a description of the believer and the church and begins with holiness. Prepare your minds, be sober-minded, be obedient children, and be holy in all your conduct, which are his instructions.

1 Peter 1:13

Prepare your minds

Peter's "therefore" is compelling. It is charged with the mercy of the Father, the guarding power of the Father, the Father's election of the saints, the sanctifying work of the Holy Spirit, the blood of Christ, his Lordship of us, a new and living hope, an imperishable inheritance, the expectation of an inexpressible joy, and the revelation of Christ with glory which even the prophets of old and angels longed to see. All this lies on the theological side leading up to "therefore," which God planned and accomplished by his mercy, grace, and power. All that the Father, the Son, and the Holy Spirit have done for the saints, Peter tells us, is the compelling reason for us to do certain things.

A mountain of doctrine has been laid upon us. Peter now tells us the response God's chosen people should naturally have: "*You shall be holy, for I am holy.*" This is our application side of Peter's "therefore," which lies in verses 15 and 16. There are other necessary things here, the tools we need by which we can live holy lives.

First, we must prepare our minds for the actions to which we are called. This is addressed in Hebrews 5:11-14. In those verses, we are told that there is an ability to discern good from evil through constant practice. A sober-minded person does this. Those who do not do so become dull and must be taught again the basic principles of the Word of God.

Second, we are to be continuously sober-minded. This is more than being right-minded because we are to be people who know the consequences of our behavior and the things that are at stake. How? There is a time and a person on which to set all your hopes; it is on the person of Christ, it is when he appears in glory, and it is on the grace that will accompany Christ in his glory, which will be poured out upon all the saints (2 Pet.3:12). If we keep this hope actively before us, we will be sober-minded and prepared for that day.

Sober-minded is spiritually-minded, for no one can set their hope on the grace of Christ unless they have spiritual discernment. Being sober-minded, as Peter is exhorting us to be, is impossible if we are not believers (2 Cor. 4:4). Even as believers, we are exhorted to exercise this gift of grace. Peter is exhorting us to focus specifically on the grace that is being poured out upon the saints to preserve them through faith until that day when Christ is revealed in the fullness of his glory,

How does the peace of God guard our hearts and minds, as mentioned in Philippians 4:7? It is by the power of God that we are guarded through faith (1 Pet. 1:5) and by having our hope set on the grace of Christ, which is to come. Paul informs us that this exercise affords us great peace of mind, which only a true believer can experience when he keeps his focus on Christ. Whether Peter tells us about the power of God guarding us through faith or Paul tells us about the peace of God guarding our hearts and minds, we are being told that God is guarding us. We call this guardianship of God the perseverance of the saints, the fifth point in the five points of Calvinism.

How can a believer lose their peace with God? The blood of Christ has propitiated God's wrath, and he is and will always be at peace with the saints. It is not this peace the question is asking about. It asks about our perception of that peace, which may become dim if we cease to focus our hope for the future on Christ and his glory. This typically occurs when we focus on our spiritual shortcomings and fail to be driven by them to Christ.

1 Peter 1:14

As obedient children

Peter's exhortations are not yet complete. Because of all God has done, we must be obedient children by forgoing all the former sinful behaviors we engaged in before being born again. In verses 1 and 2, recall that the elect were chosen by the Father and sanctified by the Spirit for obedience to Jesus Christ. Our obedience was planned; it was guarded through trials and suffering by the power of God through faith unto salvation. In addition to being planned, our obedience is the natural response of people who have become spiritually minded by the grace and power of God.

Your former ignorance

We should explore Peter's expressions in verse 14 to ensure we uncover the verse's whole meaning. He refers to our former ignorance, and we will begin with this. Our ignorance refers to the time before our eyes were open to the knowledge of the glory of Christ, when we did not recognize the divinity of his person or that he is our Lord and Redeemer. Indeed, it is a profound ignorance that is beyond correction by human wisdom and reason. It cannot be overcome or taught except by the Spirit and only to spiritually minded people (1 Cor. 2:13).

According to Peter, this time of ignorance is now over and done with, as it was a *"former"* period in which we lived. That time is over because now we are being taught by the Spirit and are now spiritually minded. But during that time, we lived in the passions that were products of that ignorance. Paul also informs us of this former life in greater detail. We walked in trespasses and sins because we were dead to the Spirit while following the spirit of the sons of disobedience and were, by nature, in body and mind, children of wrath (Eph. 2:1-3).

Peter tells us that since we no longer have the excuse of ignorance, we must no longer conform to its inherent passions. When addressing the men of Athens at the Areopagus, Paul said that God overlooked their ignorance for a time but now commands all people to repent. He went on to give a reason why they should repent. God has fixed a day of judgment by the man he appointed, and all may be assured of that because the man appointed was raised from the dead (Acts 17:30-31). Much more should we, who the knowledge of him has inwardly enlightened, be sober-minded in all spiritual things.

Since this time of ignorance is behind us, we can now live as obedient children so long as we no longer conform to the passions of our former ignorance. This is a point to pay careful attention to. Peter is saying that we are no longer ignorant, but he is not saying that the passions accompanying that ignorance have passed away. This implies that we may still yield ourselves to them and be conformed to them. The remedy lies in verse 13, which is to *"set our hope fully on the grace that will be brought to us at the revelation of Jesus Christ"* (ESV). If we do that, we will more likely not conform to the passions of our former ignorance but be *"obedient children."*

In verses 13 and 14, Peter deals with the nature of man. He delineates two times in a person's life. First, the time of former ignorance, and second, the time following. The former was marked by passions and conformity to them by which we were disobedient by nature. The latter is marked by a new ability to be obedient, having put off ignorance. Paul states this differently but with the same meaning. There is an old self and a new self. Deceitful desires corrupted the old self, but the new self has true righteousness and holiness (Eph. 2:22-24).

In a way, Peter has placed the inevitable outcome of our struggle for obedience before us. In verse 2, he wrote that we were foreknown and sanctified for obedience. The most excellent comfort of hope and assurance of faith comes to us by the Holy Spirit when we earnestly study the Word of God and seek the Spirit's illumination of truth.

Let's compare Peter to Paul (Ref. ESV).

Paul	Peter
Eph. 4:20 *But that is not the way you learned Christ!*	1 Pet. 1:12 *It was revealed to them that they were serving not themselves but you, in the things that have now been announced to you through those who preached the good news to you by the Holy Spirit sent from heaven, things into which angels long to look.*
Eph. 4:22 *to put off your old self, which belongs to your former manner of life and is corrupt through deceitful desires*	1 Pet. 1:14 *...do not be conformed to the passions of your former ignorance,*
Eph. 4:23 *and to be renewed in the spirit of your minds,*	1 Pet. 1:13 *preparing your minds for action, and being sober-minded, set your hope fully on the grace that will be brought to you at the revelation of Jesus Christ*
Eph 4:24 *and to put on the new self, created after the likeness of God in true righteousness and holiness.*	1 Peter 1:15-16 *but as he who called you is holy, you also be holy in all your conduct, since it is written, "You shall be holy, for I am holy."*

1 Peter 1:15-16

He who called is holy

So, we are to be obedient children. This begins by no longer being conformed to the lingering passions of our former ignorance and continues by striving to be holy in all we do, which is our entire conduct. Peter gives us a reason which discloses two things. First, we have been called; second, the one who called us is holy. He repeats this reason more emphatically in verse 16. We will examine both our calling and the holiness of God. Below is a list of passages on "called" and "calling."

Matt. 22:14- There is a general calling.

Rom. 1:6- There is a special calling to belong to Christ.

Rom. 1:7- Called to be saints.

Rom. 8:28- Called with God's purpose.

Rom. 8:30- Follows from being predestined.

Rom. 8:30- Leads to justification.

1 Cor. 1:9- Called into the fellowship of his Son.

1 Cor. 7:15- Called to peace.

Gal. 1:6- Called in the grace of Christ.

Gal. 5:13- Called to freedom.

Eph. 4:4- Called to one hope, the hope that belongs to your calling.

Col. 3:15- Called in one body.

1 Thess. 4:7- Called in holiness.

2 Thess. 2:14- Called through the gospel.

1 Tim. 6:12- Called to eternal life.

2 Tim. 1:9- Called to a holy calling.

Heb. 9:15- Called to receive a promised inheritance.

1 Pet. 2:9- Called out of darkness.

1 Pet. 5:10- Called to his eternal glory in Christ (also, 2 Peter 1:3).

Rom. 11:29- The calling is irrevocable.

Heb. 3:1- It is a heavenly calling.

We can organize this list by the following categories:

1. Our calling has the following characteristics:

a. it is from God with a purpose		Rom. 8:28
b. it is special, belonging to Christ		Rom. 1:6
c. it is heavenly and holy		1 Thess. 4:7
d. follows from being predestined		Rom. 8:30
e. it is irrevocable		Rom. 11:29

2. Our calling is from:

a. from outer darkness		1 Pet. 2:9

3. Our calling is to:

a. saints,	Rom. 1:7
b. eternal life,	1 Tim. 6:12
c. peace,	1 Cor. 7:15
d. a promised inheritance	Heb. 9:15
e. eternal glory in Christ	1 Pet. 5:10, 2 Pet. 1:3
f. one hope and one body	Eph. 4:4, Col. 3:15
g. freedom	Gal. 5:13
h. fellowship of the Son	1 Cor. 1:9

4. Our calling is through:

a. the grace of Christ and the gospel	Gal. 1:6

This special and holy calling by which believers have been called and which Peter refers to is not the general proclamation of the gospel, nor is it the product of common grace. We see in this calling God's love, sovereign will, grace, and power to fulfill the purpose for which he called us. Our calling is part of Peter's reason why we should live holy lives in obedience to Christ.

By the word "holy," we mean that which is pure, undefiled, righteous, incorruptible, and is entirely and utterly different from what is common. This understanding of being holy or holiness does not do justice to describing the holiness of God. We can only glimpse this subject here, but we need a better understanding of the holiness of God than just contemplating that he is different and righteous. Let's look at Isaiah 6:1-11 as our primary reference.

This is a vision given to Isaiah. It is full of symbolism, and we should realize that everything in this vision has a meaning. It is so difficult to unravel that the commentators have differences in their interpretations. Nevertheless, we can extract several elements from Isaiah 6:1-11 that are relevant to our present study. Isaiah does not behold the absolute essence of the invisible God. Instead, he is granted a manifestation of the majesty of the Lord [adonai], which he can behold. The Lord is seated as king and judge upon a throne. The throne is high and lifted up, signifying its supremacy, and Isaiah's sights of the seraphim and the altar led him to conclude he is in a temple. The edge of the Lord's robe filled the temple. Isaiah was not trying to impress us about the size of God's robe. The word "robe" is not in the original Hebrew. At the very least, Isaiah means that the very least or lowest part of God's lordship and judgeship fills the temple. One of the seraphim calls out, *"Holy, holy, holy is the Lord of hosts; the whole earth is full of his glory!"* The literal translation from the Hebrews is *"Holy of Holies holy the Lord [Yahweh] of hosts"* (see biblehub.com).

Isaiah does not see the whole of the Lord's glory because it is beyond what he can comprehend and endure. The Lord is thrice holy. This is not a simple repetition, such as holiness multiplied by three. Instead, it is holiness multiplied by holiness multiplied again by holiness. No other of God's attributes is emphasized in such a manner. All the while, the seraphim are covering their faces, for the direct vision of the Lord is too majestic and overpowering to endure. Some say they cover their feet or lower parts in humility and respect; others say they shield Isaiah from their own brightness. The "voice of him who called" is that of the Lord, for it shook *"the foundations of the thresholds."*

At the sight of the Lord [Yahweh], Isaiah realizes his uncleanness and that he lives among unclean people, so he is terrified that by seeing the Lord, he will surely be destroyed, if not already dead. Instead, Isaiah is commissioned directly by the Lord to report a devastating judgment upon the people.

We wanted to understand the holiness of God. From this passage in Isaiah, we can do so if we examine the passage from a distance and not be caught up in its details. Isaiah is being commissioned as a prophet to deliver a divine judgment. The prophecy is the foretelling of a devastating desolation to be brought upon Israel. The judgment is rendered by the holy, holy, holy Lord of hosts whose glory fills the earth. The Lord may render such judgments out of such holiness since his holiness is offended, and because he is holy, such judgments are wholly righteous.

We have read of holy men, holy angels, and holy things in scripture in such verses as Ephesians 3:5, Mark 8:33, and Joshua 6:19, for example. Revelation 15:4, from the Song of the Lamb, sheds light on this by declaring that the Lord alone is holy. If the Lord alone is holy, his holiness, as referred to in Revelation 15:4, must differ from that ascribed to created things. Thus, the seraphim call the Lord holy, holy, holy. Revelation 15:4 has an additional fact about the Lord's holiness: it is why all men fear him and glorify his name. Every reason why men worship the Lord can be traced to his holiness. What benefit would his power and knowledge be if he were not holy? What judgments might he render if he were not holy? What assurances would any of his promises convey if he were not holy?

Indeed, we have to rest in this; we cannot define the Lord's holiness apart from how his divine attributes are manifested. Holiness is the Lord's essential attribute that is attached in some way to all others. God does not lie because he is holy. God keeps his promises because he is holy. God's judgments are altogether righteous because he is holy. God is merciful and gracious because he is holy, and he is wrathful because he is holy. He uses his power for good and showers the nations with impartial providence because he is holy, holy, holy.

1:17-19 Called to be Holy Part 2 "The Precious Blood of Christ"

Having been called to be holy, Peter reminds us that it is to be pursued with fear and the knowledge that by this calling, we were ransomed with precious and imperishable things.

1 Peter 1:17-19

Calling on him as Father

Peter affirms that if you claim to know the Lord as your Father, which implies through Jesus Christ, you should act as though he is. Remember, you are in exile, living among pagans in a pagan culture that you should not be influenced by. The Lord will judge you with holy impartiality if you make a mockery of him.

If you call on him as Father, you allege you have a share in all that belongs to the saints by grace. Be mindful that if you call on him as Father, you would have been ransomed from the futile ways inherited from your forefathers. Let's pause here to examine this. Peter's logic is that if you are still living in these futile ways, you have no assurance to call God your Father and mock the ransom that you allege was paid for you. You would be alleging that the wrath of God, which you were justly under, has been propitiated and that the Father is now at peace with you on account of a ransom that was paid with the precious blood of Christ who, like a spotless lamb, was sacrificed for sin that was not his but yours.

What Peter is telling us is that because God is holy, no sober-minded person would call him Father and purposefully live an unholy life. As he says, sober-minded people ought to walk circumspectly at all times "with fear."

Election is of particular people. No one can choose to be among them. Only the specific people chosen and predestined by God for glory have been ransomed by the blood of Christ.

Suppose you are among these particular people, the elect. In that case, the only assurance you have is in an established faith marked by the fear of the Lord and a diligent effort to conduct yourself in a holy manner because these are the fruits of a transformed life under grace.

The following illustrates how precious the blood of Christ is, even when it is indirectly referenced or symbolized, particularly in the Lord's Supper. In the Lord's Supper, bread and wine are consecrated symbols of Christ's body and blood. By consecrating the bread and wine, they are set aside for the specific holy purpose Christ instituted for the church. The following demonstrates that the Lord's Supper, properly understood, is exclusively for the church and that it would be a profane use of these elements, after they have been consecrated to the Lord, for some other purpose than that for which the Sacrament was instituted. After examining the following excerpts from historic church documents and established standards of the Christian faith concerning unbelievers and the Lord's Supper, how might a church or a person demonstrate a lack of esteem or even contempt for the blood of Christ when administering the Lord's Supper?

> **The Westminster Confession of Faith Chapter 29, section 8:**
>
> "Although ignorant and wicked men receive the outward elements in this sacrament: yet they receive not the thing signified thereby, but by their unworthy coming thereunto are guilty of the body and blood of the Lord to their own damnation. Wherefore, all ignorant and ungodly persons, as

they are unfit to enjoy communion with Him, so are they unworthy of the Lord's table; and cannot, without great sin against Christ while they remain such, partake of these holy mysteries, (p) or be admitted thereunto. (q)"

(p) I Cor. 11:27, 28, 29; II Cor. 6:14, 15, 16.

(q) I Cor. 5:6, 7, 13; II Thess. 3:6, 14, 15; Matt. 7:6.

1689 Baptist Confession Chapter 30 Section 8:

"8. All ignorant and ungodly persons, as they are unfit to enjoy communion with Christ, so are they unworthy of the Lord's table, and cannot, without great sin against him, while they remain such, partake of these holy mysteries, or be admitted thereunto; yea, whosoever shall receive unworthily, are guilty of the body and blood of the Lord, eating and drinking judgment to themselves. (2 Corinthians 6:14, 15; 1 Corinthians 11:29; Matthew 7:6)"

The Westminster Confession, A Commentary by A.A. Hodge Chapter 29 Section 8:

"3. When it is said, therefore, that believers receive and feed upon the body and blood of Christ, it is meant that they receive, not by the mouth, but through faith, the benefits secured by Christ's sacrificial death upon the cross -- that this feeding upon Christ is purely spiritual, accomplished through the free and sovereign agency of the Holy Ghost and through the instrumentality and in the exercise of faith alone; so that in no case is it ever done by the unbeliever. The unbeliever, therefore, receiving the outward sign with his mouth while he fails to receive the inward grace in his soul only increases his own condemnation and hardens his own heart by the exercise. All, therefore, who are known to be unbelievers and whose unbelief is made manifest either by their ignorance or their ungodliness should be prevented, both for their own sake and for the Church's sake, from coming to the Lord's table until they are able to make a credible profession of their faith."

Westminster Larger Catechism:

"Question. 173. May any who profess the faith, and desire to come to the Lord's supper, be kept from it?

Answer. Such as are found to be ignorant or scandalous, notwithstanding their profession of the faith, and desire to come to the Lord's supper, may and ought to be kept from that sacrament, by the power which Christ hath left in his church, until they receive instruction, and manifest their reformation."

Presbyterian Church of America, Book of Church Order Chapter 58-2: "The ignorant and scandalous are not to be admitted to the Lord's Supper."

Heidelberg Catechism:

"Question 82. Are those also to be admitted to the Lord's supper who by their confession and life show that they are unbelieving and ungodly?

Answer. No, for then the covenant of God would be profaned and His wrath kindled against the whole congregation.[1] Therefore, according to the command of Christ and His apostles, the Christian church is duty-bound to exclude such persons by the keys of the kingdom of heaven, until they amend their lives."

[1] Ps. 50:16; Is. 1:11-17; I Cor. 11:17-34.

Institutes of the Christian Religion by John Calvin; Book 4 Chapter 12 Section 5: "And here, also, regard must be had to the Lord's Supper, which might be profaned by a promiscuous admission. For it is most true, that he who is entrusted with the dispensation of it, if he knowingly and willingly admits any unworthy person whom he ought and is able to repel, is as guilty of sacrilege as if he had cast the Lord's body to dogs. "

"Therefore, lest this most sacred mystery should be exposed to ignominy, great selection is required in dispensing it, and this cannot be except by the jurisdiction of the Church."

The statements above are relevant today since many churches indiscriminately offer the body and blood of Christ sacramentally to anyone. This is emblematic of the modern church's progressive drift from Biblical Christianity into the pagan culture of our time. Peter addresses how this develops and occurs in Chapter 2 of his second epistle.

1:20-21 Called to be Holy Part 3 "Christ Made Manifest"

Delving further into the nature and means of our calling, we find an overview of salvation history consisting of the Father's foreknowledge of Jesus Christ from eternity past, Christ's manifestation to the world during his incarnation, and his glorification as the risen Lord. All of this is done by the power of God, by which our faith and hope are established in God.

Jesus Christ was foreknown

Peter is continuing to exhort and encourage believers to live holy lives. His method here is to present the Father and the Son to us so that we may contemplate their glory and be moved to love and desire them. Only then may we obey the Son and live for Jesus'sake from our hearts. He presents a condensed account of God's eternal plan in these two verses (vv. 20, 21).

Verse 19 draws us to the blood of Jesus Christ. Although the preceding verses are about the Father, the antecedent of "He" with which verse 20 begins is Christ, the incarnate Son in the divine person of Jesus Christ. So, Peter is saying that Jesus Christ was foreknown before creation. It is important to understand that the Father chose us in Jesus Christ, the incarnate Son, before creation and before the incarnation of the Son (Eph. 1:3-4). Thus, the Father foreknew Jesus Christ, and not until these last times has Jesus been made manifest, which is revealed. Jesus Christ and his teaching had always been hidden until both were revealed. All that this revelation or manifesting results from is an unfolding of God's eternal plan in history, which was spoken of by the prophets (Matt. 13:35). Although the Son did not become Jesus Christ until his incarnation, which took place in history, the Father loved Jesus Christ before all time (John 17:24).

Believers in autonomous human free will should seriously consider how 1 Peter 1:20 stands in opposition to such belief by the use of the word "foreknown." The problem is that Jesus Christ was foreknown just as the elect (Rom. 8:29). God did not have to look through the corridors of time to learn who Jesus Christ would be, when he would come in the flesh, or the work he would accomplish; just as he did not have to look into the future to learn who would freely choose Jesus Christ to follow and thus elect them (Rom. 8:29, 11:2). Jesus provided a negative example of God foreknowing someone lovingly, as he loved Jesus Christ and the elect. Jesus explained, as recorded in Matthew 7:21-23 that he casts away lawless people of whom he claimed, "*I never knew you.*" But he did know they were lawless people. "Foreknow" is about God's special love that he bears exclusively for his Son and his people, the elect. The lawless people that Jesus cast away were not foreknown or loved as were the elect (Eph. 1:4-5), yet they were known to be lawless.

Peter also ties together the Father's foreknowledge of Jesus Christ with his definite plan in which lawless men delivered Jesus to be crucified (Acts 2:23). God's definite plan is rendered "*determinate counsel*" in the KJV and "*predetermined plan*" in the NASB translated from ὡρισμένη (hōrismenē) that means to determine, appoint, designate, or set boundaries and βουλῇ (boulē) that means counsel, purpose, will, plan (ref. biblehub.com). This makes it all the more compelling to apprehend God's foreknowledge as his love for Jesus and the elect since his definite plan encompasses the gospel, the covenant of grace, and election. Verse 2:8 also bears upon the free will theology, as we will see.

Jesus Christ was manifested in these last times

Peter has previously told us that the prophets of old longed to look into the things about Christ but could only see shadows and glimpses, which they could only perceive in part. During their time, Christ had not yet been manifested to them. *"In these last times,"* Christ has been manifested to us in the person of Jesus Christ.

The last times refers to the present age in history since the very last sacrifice for sin has taken place (Heb. 9:25-27), a period when the edification and discipline of God's people are through the church and a period which will be closed when Christ is revealed in his unveiled essential glory. It is a time in which the Holy Spirit dwells in believers (Acts 2:17; Rom. 8:9) and the time in which we live for whom the prophets of old wrote down their instructions (1 Cor. 10:11; Heb. 1:1-2). Things to note about the last times, days, or age:

1. There is no further sacrifice for sin.

2. God will pour out his Spirit on all flesh.

3. God speaks only through his Son.

4. We are in the last age.

1 Peter 1:21

Belief in God is through Jesus Christ

People only believe in God, specifically the Father, through the incarnate Son, Jesus. One of Jesus' great I am statements clarifies that there is only one way to come to the Father: through him (John 14:6).

God raised Jesus from the dead

In verses 20 and 21, we see glimpses of God's eternal plan.

1. The election of the Son to be Jesus Christ. Eph. 1:3-4.

2. The presentation of the savior of the world, 1 John 4:14, at the birth of Jesus.

3. The Father's calling his elect to Jesus. John 6:44

4. The resurrection of Jesus Christ by the glory and power of God. Rom. 6:4, Col. 2:12

5. The glorification of Jesus Christ. 1 Pet. 1:21

Peter regards that our contemplation of these events will cause us to recognize that our faith and hope are in God, specifically the Father, which will drive us to live holy lives. This verse draws us to the Father because Peter provides a patricentric view of God's eternal plan. The Father foreknew Jesus in verse 20. We believe in God through Jesus, but only if the Father first draws us to Jesus (John 6:44). The Father raised Jesus from the dead and gave him glory in verse 21. Furthermore, it was the Father to whom Jesus prayed to be glorified as he was before creation (John 17:5).

1:22-25 The Living and Abiding Word of God

Having been ransomed by imperishable things, previously mentioned, they are also by which we have been born again according to the word of God. Thus, Peter wants us to realize that since the word of God is eternal and imperishable, that which is through it is also imperishable.

1 Peter 1:22

Having purified your souls

Recall that it was mentioned before that Peter has a writing style in which rather than exhorting us about what to do, he commends us for practicing it. Verse 22 is a variation of this style. He has already exhorted us on what to do in the usual way of exhortation, but here, he assigns to us the actual goal of what our actions should strive for but cannot fully accomplish.

What does it mean for the soul to be purified? Peter has made two statements that shed light on this. First, in verse 14, he exhorts us not to remain conformed to the passions of our former ignorance, and in verse 18, he tells us that we have been ransomed from the futile ways inherited from our forefathers. We may then understand that a purified soul no longer conforms to previous passions and is liberated from the futile ways of their forefathers. This conclusion is justified when we consider how the soul becomes purified. According to Peter, the soul is purified by obedience to the truth, which leads to holy conduct, as stated in verse 15. Paul confirms this by telling us to do away with our former manner of life that is corrupt by deceitful desires and to live in the new way created by God after his likeness (Eph. 4:22-24). This new way is characterized by true righteousness and holiness (Eph. 2:22). Thus, we are renewed in the spirit of our minds, which is another way of expressing the purification of our souls. Being obedient to the word of God only occurs if we live in the new way God created us.

But to what characteristic of a pure soul may we look to measure the condition of our soul? We can look to brotherly love. Do we love one another with sincere brotherly love? If we do, then it is from a pure heart.

1 Peter 1:23

Born again

Just as soon as Peter, in his manner, exhorts us to exercise ourselves to purify our hearts and souls, he reminds us it is only by the mercy and power of God that this can be done. We are enabled by being born again through Jesus Christ's resurrection from the dead (1 Pet. 1:3). The cause of being born again is attributed to the Father's great mercy. But by what means do we know of God's mercy? We know of it by hearing God's word preached, the living word, which is the gospel. The gospel of Jesus Christ is the imperishable seed Peter refers to. When hearing the gospel of truth preached, we are born again if the grace of regeneration is applied to our souls. He added this to assure us that all the benefits we receive are of the Lord's mercy, power, and grace. The extent to which we have anything to do with this is only through the instrumentality of faith, a gift of grace in itself.

1 Peter 1:23-24

Our temporary earthy sojourn

This is underscored by Peter's reference to the temporal nature of our earthly existence. He references the metaphor in Isa. 40:6-8 that all flesh is like grass that withers and fades, unlike the word of God that is eternal. What we can take away is that there is no power of the flesh by which we can improve our lives in any meaningful and lasting way. He concludes with the explicit declaration that the saints have been born again by the word of God, that is, the gospel proclaimed to them.

Chapter 1 Summary

Chapter 1 of 1 Peter is a compressed yet panoramic view of salvation history in Peter's unique style. He first brought our thoughts to the Father's foreknowledge and mercy, from which he elected particular people for salvation through Jesus Christ. Thus, we were forced to contemplate things outside of time before time itself.

Peter moved us forward into our present time to cause us to reflect on our lives before we knew Christ during our former ignorance and disobedience from which the precious blood of Christ has ransomed us. There, we encountered the power of God that raised Jesus from the dead, which also raised us to spiritual life and obedience. He elevated our thoughts and emotions above the trials and sufferings of this life to the necessity of them to fulfill God's plan through which our faith secures our victory over all things as an instrument of God's mercy and power. By our faith, having been established and guarded and with a living hope, we behold the treasures of Christ: the inheritance that awaits us, being guarded in heaven and ready to be revealed when Christ is revealed in the fullness of his essential glory on the last day. A memorable passage from Chapter 1:

> *Blessed be the God and Father of our Lord Jesus Christ! According to his great mercy, he has caused us to be born again to a living hope through the resurrection of Jesus Christ from the dead, to an inheritance that is imperishable, undefiled, and unfading, kept in heaven for you, who by God's power are being guarded through faith for a salvation ready to be revealed in the last time. (1 Pet. 1:3-5 ESV)*

Chapter 2 – A Portrait of the Church

Introduction

The first half of this chapter answers, "What is the church, and who are its members?" Peter ties the answer to Christ on the one hand and our conduct on the other as members of his body. This leads to discussing the church in its visible and invisible aspects. The remainder of the chapter contains exhortations dealing with relationships. First to the government and second between servants and masters. These instructions continue into Chapter 3.

Throughout Chapter 2, there are many praises of Christ on which Peter's exhortations are founded. To know Christ is to love him, and to love him is to serve and obey him from the heart. Peter closes Chapter 2 with the following welcome-home theme, encapsulating the essence of the gospel of grace, *"For you were straying like sheep, but have now returned to the Shepherd and Overseer of your souls"* (1 Pet 2:25 ESV) What glorious assurance; I was lost, but now I am found.

2:1-3 Live Holy Lives Part 1 "Grow Up Unto Salvation"

We were previously instructed to obey the truth and earnestly love one another from a pure heart. Here, Peter lists several things the saints are to stop doing and includes an exhortation to long for spiritual growth.

Things to put away

Peter had already exhorted us to refrain from yielding to the lingering passions of our former ignorance. Verse 1 may just as well have begun with "therefore" as with "so," as there is a reason for what follows. He presents examples of traits to do away with, things we should no longer practice. We should consider this to be only a partial list of all the depraved practices of which the unregenerate human soul is, by nature, a mature and seasoned practitioner.

1. Malice—ill will toward another person. Malice is the product of two things: a debased mind and God giving one over to it. It can be accompanied by unrighteousness, evil, covetousness, envy, murder, strife, deceit, and maliciousness (Rom. 1:28-29). Paul also informs and exhorts us about malice (1 Cor. 5:8; Eph. 4:31; Col. 3:8; Tit. 3:3).

2. Deceit—deception. Deceit is evil that comes from within a person's heart and defiles them (Mark 7:21-23, Rom. 1:29).

3. Hypocrisy—false claims of higher standards or claiming to be better than you are. Jesus called out the Scribes and Pharisees for hypocrisy for making an outward appearance of righteousness when they were, in fact, lawless (Matt. 23:28). Peter was also called out for being hypocritical when he separated himself from Gentiles to associate with Judaizers

(Gal. 2:13). It's interesting that in all of Paul's epistles, there aren't any direct exhortations against hypocrisy. But in Galatians, he calls Peter out for it. Subsequently, Peter exhorts us not to be hypocrites, a demonstration of his spiritual growth.

4. Envy—a longing for or resentment for what belongs to another person or what befalls him. The psalmist likens envy to something that makes one's bones rot (Ps. 14:30). It never makes a person feel better. Pilate recognized envy as the reason the Jews wanted to hand over Jesus (Mark 27:18). Envy is also addressed in Romans 1:28-29 and 1 Timothy 6:4.

5. Slander—making false and harmful statements about someone, whether done verbally or in print, which technically is libel. Paul had much to say about slander (Eph. 4:31; Col. 3:8; 1 Tim. 3:11, 5:14, 6:4; 2 Tim. 3:3; Titus 2:3). The Corinthian church had several problems stemming from a lack of sound leadership. Consequently, Paul expected to find a host of destructive behaviors, including slander (2 Cor 12:20). Peter exhorts us to put away such behaviors so that we may live holy lives but also for the sake of the church. The very behaviors Peter lists would, among the saints, be directed against each other and threaten the unity and peace of the church. We will see how this leads to the next section in Chapter 2.

Notice that Peter is not writing in his typical style of commending the Galatians for putting these practices away. We may conclude that the Galatians needed to hear Peter's exhortation to understand its necessity. The need is just as important today for us to know that these behaviors must cease and have no place in the household of God and the hearts of believers.

1 Peter 2:2

Be like newborn infants

Peter directs us to what should replace these evil behaviors: a longing for pure spiritual milk. He is not calling the Galatian believers new believers or writing to them as if that is what he thinks of them or how they are acting. He tells us what we should be like, always ready to learn and grow spiritually. When he wrote this epistle, all of Paul's epistles and the gospel, according to Mark, had already been written, as well as James and Acts. In 2 Peter 3:16, Peter acknowledges these as inspired works and defines them as Scripture. To long for spiritual milk is his way of directing us to the inspired word.

We've come across milk in another place (Heb 5:12-14). The writer of Hebrews, likely Paul, is exhorting individuals who have not progressed spiritually, have become satisfied with the rudiments of the faith, and have left themselves in danger by not being able to discern good from evil. Whereas Peter is exhorting us, young and old, new and mature, always to long for the spiritual food of God's word as if it were pure milk so that we may continually grow and progress. However, as not all growth benefits individuals or the church, he quickly adds that this must align with salvation.

He calls believers to abandon the self-centered and self-aggrandizing practices of the old nature to become spiritually mature by the study of Scripture as a child longs for pure milk. He takes his metaphor as far as it can go by affirming that our longing for the pure word of God and spiritual maturity aligned with salvation should be like the single-minded longing of a newborn infant to be fed.

1 Peter 2:3

If you have tasted

The object of our longing ought to be the Lord Jesus Christ. If in any way we have tasted, according to Peter's metaphor, that the Lord is good, then that taste, as small as it might be, is enough to cause us to long more and more for him (Ps. 34:8).

Peter raises a hypothetical issue in verse 3, an actual warning intended to cause us to pause and examine ourselves. Either we have tasted the goodness of the Lord, or we have not. If we strive to put away the behaviors of our former nature and long for spiritual growth, we can be assured that the cause of these desires is the goodness of the Lord to us. Only then can we be assured of growing spiritually and being sanctified. If we cling to the ways of the old nature or have only a token desire for spiritual growth, we cannot be assured that we know the Lord Jesus Christ in a saving way. Living according to verses 2:1-2 is only possible if we know and love Jesus Christ and seek to know him more and more. Verse 2:3 gives the unbeliever no place of comfort among the saints.

2:4-5 Live Holy Lives Part 2 "Living Stones Being Built Up"

The apostle has set the stage for us to know that we have become different people and are to conduct ourselves differently. Peter begins a series of verses delineating the profound and essential differences between the church and the world. He starts by describing the church as a spiritual house whose members are the very materials from which this house is built. He then begins to identify church members' particular roles and duties.

1 Peter 2:4

As you come to Jesus

Peter has us contemplate the moment when we first recognized Jesus Christ. In what manner did we behold him? He presents two opposing views. The first is how the world sees Jesus—someone to be rejected. However, the way Peter phrases this rejection makes it clear that such men reject the life they need and should long for. The second view is that as seen by the Father who chose Jesus Christ for a great purpose, and he is precious to him. Peter establishes how profound this is. By writing, "*in the sight of God,*" he conveys to us that the choice of Jesus Christ and how precious he is to the Father is confirmed by sight; it is a judgment and a declaration that apart from how fallen men see Jesus, Jesus is and always will be the chosen one who saves men from their sins and is manifestly precious. For example, from Genesis 1:3-4, "*And God saw that the light was good,*" does not simply mean that God created good light or that it was good that he created it. Light demonstrates that it is good. Its goodness is confirmed by sight. In the same way, the Father knows Jesus is precious and confirms it by sight because what is inherent to Jesus is manifest to the Father.

A living stone

By referring to Jesus as a living stone, Peter uses a metaphor to convey essential concepts. God is frequently referred to as a rock. *The Lord is my rock...* (Ps. 18:2), *And who is a rock, except our God* (Ps. 18:31)? The invincible and eternal power of God to protect and secure is metaphorically described in the Psalms by denoting God as "*a rock*" and even "*my rock.*" But God's invincible power cuts two ways. For the nonbeliever, Christ is *a stone of stumbling* and *a rock of offense* (Rom. 9:33).

Paul likens Christ to the spiritual rock (1 Cor. 10:4) analogous to Peter's living stone. It is clear from Scripture that the rock upon which the church is built is Jesus Christ (Matt. 16:16-18), the cornerstone (Eph. 2:20).

A spiritual house

Simon's name, Peter, is a metaphor that Peter is transferring to Jesus and all the saints in the form of a simile. We will see in the next section that this metaphor did not originate with him. He referred to Christ as "*a living stone*" and now declares believers are "*like living stones.*" We cannot avoid the comparison Peter is making and its meaning. Believers are becoming like Jesus and are already like him in many respects. Jesus was chosen by God; believers have been chosen by God. Jesus was rejected by men, as are believers. Jesus sacrificed himself to God; believers offer spiritual sacrifices to God.

Westminster Confession	London Baptist Confession
The invisible church consists of the whole number of the elect. The visible church consists of all those throughout the world who profess the true religion, and of their children, ...	The invisible church consists of the whole number of the elect. Visible saints are all persons throughout the world, professing the faith of the gospel, and obedience unto God by Christ according unto it,...

Peter continues with this analogy. A stone building is made by cutting and shaping each stone to fit into its place. Analogously and metaphorically, he describes the saints fitted together as living stones to build a spiritual house. Since this spiritual house is the church, we properly ask if Peter is referring to the church in its visible or invisible aspects. There is one and only one Church of Jesus Christ. It exists in two aspects, visible and invisible, and is properly called the catholic or universal church. Chapter 25 of the Westminster Confession of Faith and Chapter 26 of the London Baptist Confession describe the church in these two aspects.

The WCF refers to "the visible church," whereas the LBC refers to "visible saints." The LBC does not mention the believers' children because they are not recognized as visible saints. Still, they are the offspring of the visible saints and are now holy (1 Cor. 7:14) and explicitly included in the covenantal promises of God (Acts 2:39). The word "holy" in 1 Corinthians 7:14 that is applied to the children of a believing parent is the same Greek word, ἅγιά (hagia) (biblehub.com), used in Ephesians 1:4 to refer to the elect. This does not imply that they are among the elect, but since they are holy before God, they should be regarded as holy before us. With "living stones" being fitted together into a spiritual house, does this exclude the children of believing parents who are recipients of numerous graces through the church? I think not; the visible church does include the children of believing parents, though we may not conclude that from 1 Peter alone.

According to these confessional definitions of the visible church, nonbelievers having made false professions of faith and obedience to the gospel are among the visible church. Both confessions recognize that some congregations that profess to be churches have so degenerated that they are no longer part of the kingdom of Christ and have become synagogues of Satan (WCF 25.5; LBC 26.3). As this was true when these confessions were written, so is it today.

In its full manifestation, the invisible church consists of all those chosen by God and whom only God knows who are or will be true believers united to Christ. The two confessions agree on this definition. Thus, the full manifestation of the invisible church is unchanging. However, since the visible church is not comprised of all the elect of God, neither does it consist of only the elect; it exists as a continuously changing entity. Peter is writing to and about the visible church and projecting upon it the perfections of the invisible church. While the visible church is a spiritual house, it finds its perfection only in the invisible church.

There are several important points here to take a close look at. The spiritual house is being built. We see this in progress as new believers join the church and spiritually mature. This also applies to the invisible church. Though its number remains the same, it is not presently ready to be manifested because its members must first be gathered. As to the builder, we must return to 1 Peter 1:2, where Peter writes that the Holy Spirit sanctifies. We may regard sanctification as the process by which living stones are fitted together to assemble this spiritual house, the church. Both Peter and Paul refer to the church as a house being built, Jesus Christ as a stone, and the saints forming this house (Eph. 2:19-22). Paul and Peter contribute different details to this.

Peter adds the following:

1. This is a spiritual house.

2. The members are to be a holy priesthood.

3. They will offer spiritual sacrifices to God.

4. These sacrifices are acceptable only because they are through Jesus Christ.

Paul adds the following (Eph. 2:19-22):

1. This is the household of God.

2. It is built on the foundation of the apostles and prophets.

3. It is growing into a holy temple in the Lord.

4. The Holy Spirit builds the members together.

5. This is a dwelling place for God through the Holy Spirit.

The temple of the Old Testament is, of course, where priests served and where they performed various sacrifices according to the law. In 70 AD, the Romans destroyed the second temple, which King Herod had refurbished. Such a structure has yet to be rebuilt. However, God is not without a temple. It is a holy and spiritual temple, but real nonetheless. Real sacrifices are being made spiritually and performed by a holy priesthood comprised of the saints.

As a person comes to Christ, verse 4, they come to and are joined to a spiritual house, verse 5, which is the church. Anyone who professes Christ and salvation and claims to have no part in his church is, at the very least, in error. The person who renounces the church and his membership renounces the kingdom of Christ and possibly his own participation in that kingdom.

Offering spiritual sacrifices

As to spiritual sacrifices, Peter refers to all we do in the name of the Lord to obey, honor, and glorify him. This would include mercy, kindness, generosity, defending the faith, and correcting errors with impartiality, love, and gentleness. We see in Proverbs 14 that an act of generosity honors God. Spiritual sacrifices also include all that believers do to keep themselves from evil and from doing evil things, such as resisting temptation for personal gain by being deceitful. Through Jesus Christ, the saints continuously offer spiritual sacrifices to God by acknowledging his name. Doing good and sharing what they have are pleasing sacrifices to God (Heb. 13:15-16). The spiritual sacrifices mentioned in Hebrews 13:15-16 are what we are exhorted to do, as listed in Hebrews 13:1-14, and expound what Peter refers to in verse 5.

1. Let brotherly love continue.

2. Show hospitality to strangers.

3. Remember those in prison.

4. Hold marriage in honor.

5. Keep the marriage bed undefiled.

6. Remember that God judges sexual immorality and adultery.

7. Do not love money; be content with what you have.

8. Remember your leaders and imitate their faith.

9. Do not be led away by strange and diverse teachings.

By doing these things, we offer spiritual sacrifices that are acceptable and pleasing to the Father through Jesus Christ. The offering of spiritual sacrifices is both corporate and individual. It is the household of God making them, but neither Peter nor Paul suggest that any individual is exempt.

2:6-8 Live Holy Lives Part 3 "Christ The Cornerstone"

Having been previously portrayed as a living stone, Christ is now the cornerstone. Since the saints, like living stones themselves, are being fitted together into a spiritual house, we may conclude that it is this spiritual house of which Christ is the cornerstone. Peter emphasizes Christ's rejection by the world and metaphorically describes their rejection of Christ as a stone rejected, a stone of stumbling, and a rock of offense to them.

1 Peter 2:6-8

It stands in scripture

What trust Peter expresses as he boldly declares, *"for it stands in Scripture."* The truth cannot be shaken as he recalls Isaiah 28:16. Of course, Isaiah is speaking for God, who declares that by him there is a precious cornerstone that is a tested and sure foundation laid in Zion (Isa. 28:16). Peter adds something meaningful to the Isaiah reference, the word *him* that is not found in the Hebrew text. The Greek text of 1 Pet. 2:6 does contain the word *him*. Paul does the same thing and adds *him* when he references Isaiah 28:16 (Rom. 9:33). It was veiled in the Hebrew text of Isaiah 28:16, but in Isaiah 8:14, we find the pronoun *he* is referring to a sanctuary, a stone of stumbling, and rock of offense. The metaphor has already been established in the past, as expressed through Isaiah, though partially veiled. Jesus Christ has always been the rock on which the church is built. The cornerstone is the most crucial block in a foundation. It establishes the level and layout of the foundation. Peter uses Isaiah to reinforce what he has written and, in so doing, reveals that Christ was the cornerstone for the Israelites as he is for the church since Isaiah wrote that whoever believes [on the cornerstone of a sure foundation] *"will not be in haste"* which Peter renders as *"not be put to shame."* Scripture shows Christ has always been the cornerstone of true faith and religion.

1 Peter 2:7

The honor is for you who believe

What honor is Peter referring to? It is two-fold: not being put to shame (Isa. 28:16) and having the veil lifted from our hearts and minds. For believers, the Lord is a sanctuary (Isa. 8:14). Although it was perhaps veiled to Israel that the cornerstone is a person, it could have been worked out that references to a rock were a metaphor (Isa. 8:14-15). This mystery has now been revealed to believers by which we are most honored and grateful.

Honor was previously mentioned in 1 Peter 1:7 when Christ is revealed in the fullness of his majesty. At that time, our tested faith will result in praise, glory, and honor. We should comprehend that this falls upon the saints who are revealed before the longing and hoping creation (Rom. 8:20-21).

1 Peter 2:8

Stumbling - disobey the word

The Hebrews were promised one who would establish a sure foundation (Isa. 28:16) and eternal sanctuary (Isa. 8:14; Ezek. 37:26, 28). When he came to them, they rejected him (Ps. 118:22). It seems that Paul fuses Isaiah 28:16 and 8:14 in Romans 9:32-33 where he writes that God put a stone in Zion for stumbling and offense over which the Hebrews did stumble, thus expressing a fulfillment of Isaiah 28:16. Nevertheless, Paul is expressing the same stumbling over Jesus Christ by the Jews and non-believers as does Peter.

As they were destined to do

However, Peter discloses why people rejected Christ. They stumbled over him because they rejected the word, that is, Scripture. Then he writes something remarkable: they rejected Christ and the word of God because they were destined to do so. The Greek word being translated as *destined* is ἐτέθησαν (etethēsan), which may be translated as *appointed* (biblehub.com) as it is in the KJV and NASB. The root meaning of this is to fix or establish. So, why did the non-believers stumble over the precious cornerstone, Jesus? Was it because they disobeyed the word (Scripture), as verse 8 states, or because God appointed them to stumble, as the verse also states? Peter's clear, unambiguous meaning is that people reject Christ because God destined or appointed them to reject him. Although they were graciously given God's word, they disobeyed it, and God's appointed outcome followed.

This brings up the issue of reconciling God's sovereignty and man's responsibility, which many stumble over by concocting various schemes of explanation. We should accept that God is sovereign and man is responsible at the same time without contradiction. Speculation should be avoided. In light of verse 8, we need to recognize that some nonbelievers may be among the elect and will come to faith in God's time and by his grace. But until such time, they remain under the decree that Peter stipulates and will continue to disobey Scripture and stumble over Jesus as they are unable to will otherwise.

1 Peter 2:8 opposes the belief that individuals can freely choose to follow Jesus Christ. Since nonbelievers were appointed to disobey the gospel, no amount of human free will can produce a different outcome. When Adam sinned against God, God decreed the conditions into which Adam and his descendants fell. The conditions God established comprise spiritual inability, corruption, and hopelessness that are manifested by spiritually stumbling and disobeying the gospel. Nothing changes for nonbelievers whose unavoidable outcome is perishing (John 3:16) unless they are foreknown and chosen by the Father, who intervenes with saving grace for obedience to Jesus Christ in the sanctification of the Holy Spirit (1 Pet. 1:2). Surely, anyone who rejects Jesus Christ as Lord and Savior will perish unless they begin to

believe (John 3:16), but who can believe who has been destined to perish? The Father must call you for you to become a saint (Rom. 1:7; 1 Cor. 1.2), deliver you from the domain of darkness (Col 1:13), draw you to Jesus Christ (John 6:44), call you out of darkness into his marvelous light (1 Pet. 2:9), and deliver you from the corruption that is in the world (2 Pet. 1:4). Until he does, and you are born again (John 3:3, 5), it remains as Jesus said, *"No one can come to me..."* (John 6:44). Praise God for all who believe, who have been appointed to eternal life (Acts 13:48) and assigned a measure of faith (Rom. 12:3).

2:9-12 Live Holy Lives Part 4 "Sojourners and Exiles, but God's People"

Peter uses these verses to instill in believers the reality of who and what we are. Although nonbelievers will speak against us as evildoers, we are instructed to guard our conduct among them because of who we are. Thus, some nonbelievers may glorify God after seeing our good deeds.

1 Peter 2:9

A chosen race

Peter is writing to Jews who have become faithful believers in Christ. They grew up in the Hebrew faith but without a temple, temple sacrifices, or a priesthood to practice it. Peter has been and continues to explain to them that the former things were types and shadows of what has now come. They and all believers are a chosen race; God has not abandoned them. In this, there is an allusion to election.

The word "race" is used figuratively and is explained by what follows. First, believers have been chosen to be a royal priesthood. Peter is drawing upon the Old Testament. When the people of Israel had come to Mount Sinai and encamped, God spoke to Moses on the mountain and told him that upon obedience, the people would be "*a kingdom of priests and a holy nation*" (Exod. 19:5-6). That promise, as trustworthy as it was, did not fully materialize for the Israelites because of their disobedience. However, because God was faithful to his promise, the promise materialized through Jesus Christ, by his obedience and the calling of individuals chosen by God. And, of course, believers are priests because we offer spiritual sacrifices to God through Jesus Christ. Because they were descendants of Abraham, the mindset of being a chosen people had been a part of Jewish culture. However, Abraham was not promised this of his descendants, but one descendant, Christ (Gal. 3:16). God's people are only chosen through Christ, and only through Christ do people become a holy nation. Although the nation of Israel was disobedient, God kept a remnant to himself even in the worst of times (1 Kings 18:18).

Although believers are scattered across the world, speak many different languages, and embrace diverse cultures, we are unified as one body by one Spirit, called to one hope, one Lord, one faith, one baptism, one God and Father (Eph. 4:4-6). Thus, believers may rightly be called one nation or even one race. In addition, we are a royal priesthood because we offer spiritual sacrifices to God through Jesus Christ (1 Pet. 1:5; Heb. 13:15), who is king over all (Rev. 1:5, 17:14).

Called out of darkness

God desires that believers proclaim his excellencies, that is, to glorify him. Just as God's invisible attributes are manifested in creation (Rom. 1:20), so are his excellencies manifested by his chosen people.

Peter reminds us that God called us out of the darkness, our former lives of disobedience, misery, and ruin, and into his marvelous light, whereby we have come to Jesus. By being called out of darkness, we escaped the corruption that is in the world (2 Pet. 1:4). This corruption and darkness involved sexual immorality, impurity, passion, evil desire, and covetousness, which is idolatry (Col. 3:5). These and more like them are the works of the flesh by which no person can enter the kingdom of God (Gal. 5:19-21). But praise be to God, for he called us out of darkness. He didn't call to give us a choice or provide a way to extricate ourselves from the darkness and corruption. His call effectually delivered us from the bondage of darkness and transported us into the kingdom of his Son (Col. 1:13) and "into his marvelous light."

In Jude verse 6, we are told that angels who sinned are kept in eternal chains of gloomy darkness until judgment. Similarly, the natural man is held captive by the darkness he is in. Only by the Father's drawing him to Jesus Christ (John 6:44) is the natural man released from darkness to escape the corruption that is in the world (2 Pet. 1:4).

1 Peter 2:10

Now you are God's people

Before we were called, we were not a recognizable group of people, had not received mercy, and lived with the consequences of our depravities. But now we have been called, received mercy, and are God's people. Because of his mercy and calling to us, we should be driven to glorify God and be thankful. Our thankfulness to God should be manifest in how we live our lives (Eph. 5:8).

1 Peter 2:11

Sojourners and exiles

Peter goes on to plead with believers, whom he calls beloved because they are precious to the Father, to abstain from the passions of the flesh. He even pleaded with the saints, even the most pious, to abstain from the passions of the flesh because none of us is immune from them, and unless we engage in their warfare against us, we will surely be overcome and give in to them. Put them off, do away with them, even put them to death. To indulge them demonstrates ingratitude toward the grace you may claim to have received and mocks God's mercy. Peter knows what is at stake and engages all his efforts to hold us back from our former ways. He says these passions wage war against our souls; they seek to ruin us and fill us with regret, guilt, and misery. If we continue to practice these things, we will surely suffer the loss of any assurance of faith.

We are exhorted to maintain honorable behavior in all that we do, not what the world or the present culture regards as honorable, but that which honors God. Although it may cause some people to say evil things to and about you, your honorable behavior toward the Lord may be the impetus for some to glorify God. Jesus referred to his coming in the flesh to Israel as *"the time of your visitation"* (Luke 19:44), a special visitation to the nation. Still, the day, Peter mentions, is more personal when the Spirit comes to a person and either abides or passes by. The Spirit may use your good behavior to prepare a man's soul for that day. However, I suggest there is another aspect to Peter's words, which is how God may be glorified. By seeing the saints' good deeds and reviling the saints for them, heaps more wrath upon the reprobate by which God is glorified when his righteous judgment comes upon them.

It may seem that Peter has left something out. How might the saints be able to do what we are being exhorted to do? However, verse 9 tells us that we have been brought *"into his marvelous light"* and thus are now children of light (Eph. 5:8; 1 Thess. 5:5). Thus, as children of light, we may cast off the works of darkness (Rom. 13:12).

Peter reminds the Jews to whom he is writing that their citizenship is not of this world but that they are passing through as sojourners. Their citizenship is in heaven, and they should be careful not to jeopardize their assurance by living as if they are still in the world. As for the saints today, they should be cautious as this warning applies to everyone.

Keep your conduct honorable

Peter understands the influences of a pagan culture. He exhorts us always to behave in ways that honor our Lord. We should respond with good works when spoken of as evildoers, presumably for our faith (Rom. 12:19-21). Later, he tells us to bless those who are evil to us (1 Pet. 3:9). By blessings and good works to those who are cruel to us; we may heap burning coals on their heads (Rom. 12:20), a metaphor for a guilty conscience. He takes this further by saying this may lead to their conversion.

Peter has told us essential things about true believers in Christ. True believers have previously been chosen by God. Though they were once in darkness, they have been called into his marvelous light and have received mercy. Here is a brief review of what he has told us.

1. True believers have been chosen by God.

2. They were once in darkness and without mercy.

3. God has called them into his marvelous light.

4. Believers were not a people but now are a chosen race.

5. They are a royal priesthood, offering spiritual sacrifices to God.

6. They are a holy nation of people for God's possession.

7. All of this would not have been possible if believers had been on their own and God had not called them

from darkness into light.

8. The passions of the flesh remain at war against our souls.

2:13-17 Submission to Authority Part 1 "Subject to Human Institutions"

With verse 13, Peter starts a lengthy section on submission to authority that extends into Chapter 3. He begins by addressing the saints in general and how they should conduct themselves concerning the secular world and the institutions surrounding them. His address to servants follows, and the chapter concludes with a discourse on Christ the Good Shepherd, whose obedience and suffering on our behalf are the reasons we should submit to authority to honor God.

1 Peter 2:13-14

Be subject for the Lord's sake

First, we must deal with what Peter means by "*human institutions.*" God orders and rules all human affairs so that men everywhere are under his dominion. Peter does not mean or imply there are institutions built and operated by men that in any way are exempt from God's sovereign rule. He refers to the human institutions that do not recognize God's dominion over them or his right to govern them (Ps. 47:8). Though they deny him, he governs them. Though they oppose him, he uses them (Dan. 5:21).

A principal reason why Peter exhorts believers, particularly Jews of his day, to submit to human institutions is to deny their leaders the reason and opportunity to become more oppressive. Also, civil authorities perceived that the new spiritual freedom enjoyed by Christians posed a threat to their authority. Nothing has changed in 2000 years. So, Peter's exhortation lies in this truth that those who regard you as a potential problem need little provocation to use their authority against you. By submitting to them, you will not provoke them, the faith can go forward, and you will honor Christ.

The crux of our submission to human instructions and their leaders is so that we do not give them any reason or cause to think that the power of God is of no effect or is a fiction of our minds and by such conduct disgrace the Lord, as Peter phrases it, *"for the Lord's sake."*

1 Peter 2:15

The will of God

Peter reminds us that his words are God's words. It is the will of God that we should act in a good manner to all civil authority, and in so doing, we will shut their mouths against us and bring no shame upon the Lord. He discloses that the proper function of civil authority is to punish the evil and reward the righteous. However, more often than not, the reverse occurs, and when that is the case, Christians are more likely to be opposed and put upon. We can silence their ignorance with our good deeds in response to them.

1 Peter 2:16

Live as people who are free

Peter draws our attention to our wonderful freedom in Christ and instructs us not to abuse it. We have not been granted the license to do whatever we please with our bodies in the name of freedom. He does not imply that covering up evil with our freedom is possible because, though Peter does not specify, God discerns the thoughts and intentions of the heart (Heb. 4:12-13). He immediately reminds us to live as servants of God to prevent us from thinking so.

1 Peter 2:17

Honor everyone

In verse 17, Peter lists four brief exhortations. The one that immediately stands out is *"fear God."* According to Proverbs, the fear of the Lord is described as follows:

1. The fear of the Lord is the beginning of knowledge (1:17).

2. The fear of the Lord is hatred of evil (8:13).

3. The fear of the Lord is the beginning of wisdom (9:10).

4. The fear of the Lord prolongs life (10:27).

5. In the fear of the Lord, one has strong confidence (14:26).

6. And his children will have a refuge (14:26).

7. The fear of the Lord is a fountain of life (14:27).

8. By the fear of the Lord, one turns away from evil (16:6).

Critical to our understanding of fearing the Lord lies in Proverbs 9:10. If a person is to be wise, he must first fear the Lord. Even then, he is not wise; he only begins to be wise. The opposite is also true. Someone who does not fear the Lord has no wisdom. This is not referring to a body of knowledge that can be recalled and recited. It's referring to two things. First, all actual knowledge is understood in its relationship to God. To know something as God knows it is actual knowledge. Isn't it true that as we study the Bible and learn about God, we increasingly see ourselves as God sees us: what we were, what we are, and what we shall become? Second, the one who has wisdom, in the fear of the Lord, is able to use his true knowledge with insight to live righteously and please God (Prov. 9:10).

We love to love fellow believers, but we may suffer sorrowful hurt and injuries from the saints in our own congregations. When this happens, we still are to love those who cause us pain. We are even called to honor those who may cause us great sorrow from outside the church. And even those in positions who caused us unimaginable harm are to be honored. Our focus needs to be on our duty to honor whoever we contact or speak about rather than what they have done or could do to us, keeping in mind that their actions toward us are part of God's eternal plan. In his continual style of brevity, Peter provides consolation for the difficulties of honoring those who abuse and despise us. We are to fear the

Lord. That fear and what it provides is relevant in this context (Ps. 34:9.) Those who fear the Lord will lack nothing.

Paul sums it up another way, based on the fear of God and faith in his promises. Cleansing or putting off every defilement of the body and spirit leads to holiness (2 Cor. 7:1).

In summary, we need to see Peter's exhortation to honor others in light of the psalmist and Paul and his writing context. He brings us out of our comfort zone and into the realm of human institutions that harbor antipathy toward Christ and his church. The will of God for us is to honor him with our conduct. We proceed by fearing the Lord, without which we will have no success. He governs all human institutions, no matter how secular they claim to be. Our responsibility is to submit to their rule over us so long as it does not lead us to disobey God. Doing this makes us less likely to stir up antipathy toward the church, which may lead to difficulties. Even when difficulties arise, our calling is to honor those who afflict us.

2:18-20 Submission to Authority Part 2 "Submission to Masters"

Continuing with the theme of submission to authority, Peter turns our attention to servants. It is probably not correct to render the particular Greek word οἰκέται (oiketai) as "slave" but rather as "servant."

1 Peter 2:18

Servants, be subject to your masters

The Greek word φόβῳ (phobō) is translated as fear, with fear, terror, or fears 41 times and as respect 3 times in Scripture, according to Strong's information. Why is it rendered as respect here? I consider it depends to whom the fear or respect is being paid. If a servant is to be subject to his master in the fear of God, then *phobō* should be rendered as fear, as it is in the KJV and NIV Bibles. However, if it is considered that the submission to the master is to be conducted with *phobō* to the master, it could be rendered as respect as it is in the ESV and NASB to maintain harmony with the tenor of verse 18. Either way, this is understood to result in the same final exhortation. All the saints, including believing servants, are to honor everyone, including masters. All the saints, including believing servants, are to fear God. An important thing to point out is that Peter writes that a servant's submission to their master is to be with *all* fear or with *all* respect so that the servant is to hold nothing back in either case.

As not all masters are good and gentle, the temptation exists for servants to be insubordinate to unjust and cruel masters. Peter is clear that the harshness of a master is not an excuse to be disobedient. A servant is to be subordinate regardless of whether his master is good or harsh. These principles apply to the modern workplace and employees.

1 Peter 2:19-20

Being mindful of God while suffering

Peter goes on to encourage servants, particularly those whose masters are unjust. He writes that submission amid such suffering is gracious when endured out of a good conscience toward God. A gracious thing is also an acceptable thing.

He elaborates that there is no credit or reward if a servant is punished for their faults and continues to serve in the same manner. But when a servant is harshly treated and suffers when doing good to his master, God sees his continued good service as grace. It is gracious to serve under such circumstances, and God confirms it by sight.

2:21-23 The Good Shepherd Part 1 "The Suffering Shepherd"

Peter explains that we have been called to submit to all authority over us, leading us back to Christ as our reason and example. We are given a brief but rich view of Christ's submission during suffering, its conditions, and his response. Verse 22 catches our attention because it is theologically rich in meaning, and we will spend some time pursuing it.

1 Peter 2:21

Called to follow in Christ's steps

Peter explains the underlying reality behind all godly submissions and the circumstances of it. God ordained it, and the saints have been called to it. Peter's words are not a general statement about being called to the general work of service and submission but to the actual specific details of the situation and circumstance one finds himself in as part of God's eternal plan. In the first chapter, he has already shown the necessity of all we endure as part of God's eternal plan. Even though there are necessary but grievous trials, they are only for a short while (1 Pet. 1:6). As there is a purpose for various trials, there is a purpose in submission and service, which are done for the sake of Christ.

Leaving you an example

Peter immediately ties our calling to submission and service to Christ and presents Christ to us as an example of obedience and suffering. Christ's suffering was for us so that the calling by which we have been called would be effectual for the purpose appointed by God. By expressing this to us, Peter presents Christ as the example we should follow and the most compelling reason for our submission. As the Son exercised all obedience to his calling to suffer for us, so should we be obedient for his sake to our calling. Peter leaves us no room to argue against God's justice in these matters. The apostle Paul provides an example of personal suffering and submission for the sake of Christ. Gaining the knowledge of Jesus Christ as Lord was worth the personal loss of all things (Phil. 3:8).

Peter tells us to follow in Christ's footsteps and begins a glorious discourse on Christ. He makes the following claims about Jesus Christ in the following order:

1. He suffered for you. ("You" are the Galatian Jews who now believe, and by extension, all believers. "You' is the plural, collective form.)

2. He left you an example of himself to follow.

3. He committed no sin.

4. He did not utter deceit.

5. When reviled, he did not revile in return.

6. When he suffered (presumably unjustly by human hands), he did not threaten (retaliate).

7. He bore our sins and was physically crucified so that you would die to sin.

8. By his wounds, you are healed.

9. He is the Shepherd and Overseer of your souls.

Peter's logic is that we should copy Christ from our hearts because Christ has done all this for us. We should not sin, deceive, revile, or retaliate but trust and honor God.

It would be wrong of us to think that Christ's sufferings are all the suffering that there should be and that the saints, having received his grace, should not have to suffer. Paul recognizes that his own suffering is for the sake of the church and ties his suffering to that of Christ (Col. 1:24). As Christ's afflictions were ordained for the church, so are the afflictions of the saints. Though when we suffer, it may not be in the performance of some great ministry to the church, as was Paul's, it is nonetheless necessary as it is an inseparable part of God's eternal plan, as are all things for the sake of his glory and the church.

1 Peter 2:22

He committed no sin

In verse 22, Peter states, "*He committed no sin.*" Although he is writing within the immediate contextual framework of suffering, his words about Christ are universally true. Christ committed no sin that he should be made to suffer, but Christ absolutely committed no sin.

How does this fact about Christ reconcile with his human nature? The guilt of Adam's original sin was imputed to the entire human race (Rom. 5:12; Ps. 51:5). So if death spread to all men as claimed in Romans 5:12, why doesn't it apply to Jesus? From the Westminster Confession of Faith:

> They [Adam and Eve] being the root of all mankind, the guilt of this sin was imputed and the same death in sin, and corrupted nature, conveyed to all their posterity descending from them by ordinary generation (WCF 6:3).

Let's examine how Adam came to be. The Lord formed Adam from the dust of the ground and breathed life into him, making Adam a living creature (Gen. 2:7). As to flesh, there are many different kinds as God has chosen, but only one kind for humans (1 Cor. 15:37-39). Accordingly, all the descendants of Adam are of the same "kind" as Adam: fallen, corrupt, and sinful. This applies to anyone of the seed of Adam; they bear his image.

There is a clear distinction between Adam and Jesus. Adam was from the earth, a man of dust. And like Adam, so are all his descendants according to the principle of seed and kind (1 Cor. 15:37-39). But Jesus is not from the earth; he is from heaven. Adam was the man of dust, and Jesus is the man of heaven (1 Cor. 15:45-49). As to the incarnation, Jesus was not descended from Adam by ordinary generation. The Holy Spirit came upon Mary who became pregnant with Jesus, the Son of God (Luke 1:35). Jesus was not conceived in Mary from a man who was of the Adamic kind, but from the Holy Spirit (Matt. 1:20). Indeed, he is from heaven and does not bear the image of Adam. Thus, there is no imputation of original sin or conveyance of a corrupt nature. The child born, Jesus, is holy (Luke 1:35; Matt. 1:20).

We should clarify why Adam is called the first man, and Jesus is called the second man and the last Adam. As we have seen, only two men have come into the world without sin and corrupt natures: Adam and Jesus. Adam was made from the dust of the earth, and Jesus was from the Holy Spirit, and they were both fully human, without sin, holy and righteous. In that respect, Adam is a type of Jesus (Rom. 5:14), but Adam is also a type of Jesus who is a representative person. Adam represented the whole human race, so whatever Adam did was legally applied to all his descendants. Thus, when Adam fell into sin and corruption, the entire human race fell with him. Similarly, Jesus is a representative person but not of the whole human race. Jesus is the federal head of the church, particularly the elect only. Thus, what Jesus did was legally applied to the church, the elect of God. The concepts of 1 Corinthians 15:45-49 about all men bearing the image of Adam results from Adam's federal headship over all men. In contrast, only the elect bear the image of Jesus as he is their federal head. Finally, Jesus is called the last Adam because there is no part in God's eternal plan for any further succession of federal headship.

1 Peter 2:23

When he was reviled

At some time during his earthly ministry, Jesus Christ was imputed with the guilt of all the sins of the elect. It doesn't appear in Scripture that we can know precisely when that occurred. Even after it was imputed to him, Jesus Christ never sinned or deceived anyone. Why do I bring this up? Because Jesus died the death that was judiciously and righteously due to anyone guilty of sin, including the Son of God. But until our guilt was laid upon him, the suffering of death for sin had no claim on him.

Now, we come to the point Peter is making. Throughout his earthly ministry, Jesus suffered many times and in many ways at the hands of men, and since he had no sin and had not the guilt of ours laid upon him until later, he suffered unjustly. During that time, as he suffered unjustly, he did not revile or threaten but entrusted himself to God.

Even later, during his time before the Sanhedrin and Pilate, Jesus was unjustly handled, charged, prosecuted, convicted, sentenced, and executed by men. Here, we delineate between men and God. Man's justice was corrupted by envy, hate, malice, and pride. God's justice was holy and righteous following the imputation of the guilt of our sin; *"For the wages of sin is death..."* (Rom. 6:23). Scripture informs us how unjustly evil men treated Jesus. Jesus was falsely accused (Mark 15:3), beaten (Luke 22:63), derided (Mark 15:29), spat upon (Matt. 26:67), and was eventually flogged (John 19:1). When he was crucified, even the robbers crucified on either side reviled him (Matt. 27:44).

We are told in verse 21 that Christ gave us an example of how to cope with suffering. But we need to see this from the correct perspective. We are told that Christ suffered for us, from which we should understand that the purpose of Christ's suffering was for our benefit. It is grievous when we suffer, especially when we see no purpose. But now, even though we may not see a purpose, we should know that our suffering does have a purpose. We are keenly aware of the differences between suffering unjustly and justly for our faults. Of Christ, Peter informs us that he had no sin, no deceit in his mouth, and he did not revile or threaten others, which was his response to unjustly suffering. He entrusted himself to God. There was no fault in Jesus that he should be made to suffer, and there was no fault in Jesus due to his suffering. Since Christ suffered unjustly for us, when we suffer, we should do so as Christ did, without deceit, reviling, threatening, or sin. Just as Christ did, we should entrust ourselves to God, referring our suffering to God, who will bring a just outcome to all things.

2:24-25 The Good Shepherd Part 2 "The Shepherd Who Bore Our Sins"

Verse 24 needs careful investigation. Examining the circumstances that led and enabled Jesus to bear our sins could fill volumes, so we will settle for an overview of several doctrinal topics that will provide a thorough overview of how and why the saints needed to be redeemed and how and why Jesus Christ came to be our redeemer. It is edifying to do this to fully understand the underlying truths of what Peter has written, the facts on which it is founded that are beneath the words of the verse, and make the verse stand as a paramount confession of our faith.

1 Peter 2:24

He bore our sins

These four tiny words are packed with an enormous amount of theology that we will endeavor to unpack. A student driver's first lesson does not involve explaining how an internal combustion engine works. But whether you are a new or longtime believer, reviewing the Biblical basics of our faith is profitable to avoid false presuppositions and errors or drifting into error.

Jesus is the Christ, the Son of God in the flesh, fully human and fully God, a divine person full of grace (John 1:14.) He is the only one in the whole of Scripture described as being full of grace, and we must take that to mean that at all times he was full of grace, continuously. All we are and ever will be is by God's grace through Jesus Christ. By God's grace, we have a Savior who has done what we cannot do for ourselves by satisfying the demands of the law (Luke 24:44; Rom. 8:4) and taking upon himself the due punishment for our sins (Rom. 1:27, 5:9, 8:1; 1 Thess. 1:10, 5:9.)

This first phrase in verse 2:24 results from conditions embedded in God's eternal plan (Acts 2:23.) It would be beneficial to explore how and why Jesus bore our sins as we seek to understand its full significance.

Predestined for adoption—When we examine God's eternal plan, we see that it begins with God's love for people who are to be a chosen race (Eph. 1:3-4; 1 Pet. 2:9.). They are the elect and are predestined for adoption as sons of God through Jesus Christ (Eph. 1:5.) Many things must happen for that predestined adoption to be a reality.

Federal headship—Federal headship is a crucial part of God's plan. A federal head is a person who legally represents all persons, past, present, and future, of the same "kind." A federal head is also called a representative person. This is not like the representation of a lawyer. In the beginning, Adam was the federal head of all mankind, but, as we will see, this was to change for some people. What a person does as a federal head is imputed to all persons under his headship, just as if they had done it themselves, whether for good or evil. Additionally, the nature or image of a federal head is the nature or image of all persons under his federal headship. Under Adam's federal headship, his nature or image is passed on to the rest of mankind by ordinary generation, physical birth (1 Cor. 15:49; c.f. Eph. 2:3.) Therefore, his descendants, having the exact nature as him, are of the same kind and bear the same fallen and corrupt image.

Adam's fall produced two barriers—Adam is called the first man (1 Cor: 15:45), referencing his federal headship. When he sinned, all mankind sinned with him and died (Rom. 5:12; 1 Cor. 15:22.) This was spiritual death (Eph. 2:1.) So, due to Adam's "fall," mankind finds itself inexorably subject to the wrath of God (Rom. 6:23.) His fall places two barriers between man and God. First, we have a body of sin for which we must suffer the judgment of God and perish (Rom. 2:5, 5:16.) Second, due to our corrupt nature (Eph. 2:3; 1 Cor. 15:49), we are unable to fulfill the law (Rom. 2:12).

The last Adam—However, since there is a "first Adam," there must also be a "second Adam" who is referred to as the "last Adam" (1 Cor. 15:45.) By employing the name Adam, federal headship is referred to and by referring to the second Adam as the last Adam we see that federal headship does not progress further to a subsequent person. Who is this "last Adam?" He is from heaven (1 Cor. 15:47) and can only be Jesus Christ.

The incarnation of Christ—This brings us to the incarnation of God's Son, Jesus Christ. He was conceived in the womb of Mary by the Holy Spirit (Matt. 1:18, 20), born in the likeness of men (Phil. 2:7), and born under the law (Gal. 4:4.) It is essential to understand that Jesus Christ is a divine person with two natures. His human nature is derived through Mary but not by ordinary generation. It is thereby without sin, and its corruption (Heb. 4:15.) The Son was from all eternity the second person of the Trinity who took on a mortal body of flesh and human nature to become Jesus Christ, being both man and God. There is no confusion between Christ's divine nature and human nature, although they are eternally inseparable. We can speak of one person, Jesus Christ, who has two natures but is always and only a divine person. Being born in the flesh (Rom. 8:3; 1 Tim. 3:16; Heb. 5:7; 1 Pet. 4:1; 1 John 4:2; 2 John 1:7) and under the law (Gal. 4:4), Christ is now qualified to fulfill his purpose according to the Father's eternal plan by being the new federal head of God's elect and bring down the two barriers that separate the elect from God which he can now do having our nature and being without sin (Heb. 4:15).

The elect transferred to Christ—Adam remains the federal head for many people. But for some, God has transferred them to the federal headship of his Son (Col. 1:13), removing them from Adam's federal headship. Until that transfer occurs, a person has two insurmountable problems that separate him from God. As Christ is the federal head of the elect, the chosen race, what he accomplishes is legally counted, or imputed, to them as if they had done so themselves.

Jesus Christ, the divine person, can suffer death—To fulfill God's plan of redemption, Christ must die. The Son, being God, cannot die because he is eternal (Deu. 33:27; Rom. 16:26; Heb. 9:14; 1 Pet. 5:10). But now, through his incarnation, the person Jesus Christ has a mortal body of flesh and can die.

With a physical body, Jesus Christ can be nailed to the cross and die. This is what Christ did; he submitted to being brutalized and nailed to the cross to suffer death. Having a physical body and human nature, we can correctly say that Christ, the divine person, died (Rom. 5:6,8; 1 Cor. 8:11, 15:3; 1 Cor. 5:14). Throughout his death, there was no separation or disunity of his two natures.

Living under the law without sin and qualified to be the sacrificial lamb of God—To fulfill God's plan of redemption, Christ's death must be sacrificial for sin. Christ could not die as an acceptable sacrifice for sin until he had first lived under the law without sin. Being born under the law and without sin, he had to obey the law without spot or blemish (1 Pet. 1:19). This necessitated that there was no guilt of sin found in him by commission, omission, thought, or deed. Spot or blemish is a reference to sacrifice. The only acceptable sacrifice is without a spot or blemish. By living under the law in perfect obedience, Jesus became qualified to be the sacrificial lamb of God (John 1:29, 36).

Our guilt was imputed to Christ—Some may ask, how might we be sure Jesus had no sin of his own? To answer, we examine his sacrifice. When a Levitical priest offers the annual sacrifice for sin, he must first sacrifice a bull for his own sin before sacrificing a goat for the people's sins. Jesus made no such sacrifice for his own sins because he had none. Otherwise, his sacrifice would not have been acceptable. Since Jesus committed no sin, was Jesus innocent when he died, and was his death an injustice? He was not guilty of violating any laws, civil or otherwise. He committed no legal offense. Therefore, it was unjust for men to make him suffer and kill him. Peter called them lawless men (Acts 2:23), but it was according to God's design for Jesus to suffer and die (Acts 2:23). We must realize that while Jesus died physically at the hands of lawless men, his death was more than just a physical death. The full measure of God's wrath was poured out upon him, the satisfaction of eternal punishment (Isa. 53:5; Matt. 25:46). Since God will not condemn an innocent person, he must become legally guilty of sin to suffer God's wrath before he could justly be put to death. That was accomplished by imputing the whole body of sin, past, present, and future, of the elect and only of the elect to him. Our guilt of sin was wholly imputed to Jesus (Isa. 53:12; Col. 2:14), and he became legally subject to God's justice (Rom. 6:23). Indeed, the Son of God bore our sins, was legally found guilty, numbered among the sinners (Isa. 53:12; Luke 22:37), and suffered the wrath of God. Only our guilt was imputed to Christ, not our corrupt nature, and while this constituted him guilty before God, it did not constitute him a sinner.

The Lord Jesus Christ died for our sins—Jesus' death was an actual physical death. He died (1 Pet. 3:18; Acts 10:39; Rom. 5:8, 8:34; 1 Thess. 4:14; 1 John 3:16), gave up his spirit (Mark 27:50; John 19:30), and his body was laid in a tomb (Mark 15:46; Matt. 27:59-60; Luke 23:53; John 19:42). Christ's divine nature is crucial, for death couldn't hold him (Acts 2:24), yet the judicial demand of eternal punishment was met. No mere man could have been qualified as Jesus was or could have accomplished what Jesus accomplished for the elect. We know this to be true because Jesus Christ was bodily raised from among the dead (Matt. 27:64; John 2:22; Act 3:15, 13:30; Rom. 6:9; 1 Cor. 15:20), and God remains righteous and just (Rom. 2:26). No mere man was crucified, it was the Lord Jesus Christ nailed there (1 Cor. 2:2; Mark 15:32; Acts 2:36; Gal. 3:1).

Fulfilling the law—The elect, previously under Adam's headship, had two insurmountable barriers between them and God. They could not perfectly obey the law themselves. Jesus dealt with this barrier, in part, by living a perfect life under the law for the elect as their federal head. He accomplished this before being crucified, qualifying him as an acceptable sacrifice. He lived his entire life in strict and perfect obedience to God's law, but he did not fulfill the entirety of the law until he was crucified and died. Under the law of sin, the elect owed the debt of death to God (1 Cor. 15:56). The wages of sin is death (Rom. 6:23), and that is a legal demand (Col. 2:14). When Jesus Christ died on the cross, the demands of the law, the entire body of law, were fulfilled. This is known as Jesus Christ's forensic righteousness, which was legally established by fulfilling the law. This must not be confused with Christ's intrinsic righteousness, which belongs exclusively to God. In fulfilling the law, it was not only the moral law but also the sacrificial law that required a perfect sacrifice and a high priest. Jesus was both the perfect sacrifice by obedience and high priest according to promise and by oath (Ps. 110:4; Heb. 7:28). Additionally, Jesus had to be a qualified kinsman redeemer to propitiate God's wrath and ransom his people (Matt. 1:2-16; Luke 3:23-38; Heb. 2:17).

Brought into the kingdom of the Lord Jesus Christ— God transfers the elect from Adam's headship to Christ's when he delivers them, individually, from the bondage of darkness to the kingdom of his beloved Son (Col. 1:13). It begins by being born again (John 3:3,7; Gal. 4:29; 1 Pet. 1:3, 23), also known as regeneration (Titus 3:5). The person born again is a new creation (2 Cor. 5:17; Gal. 6:15), changed inwardly (Ezek. 36:26; Eph. 4:24; Col. 3:10) by the working of divine power (2 Pet. 1:3) and grace (2 Cor. 9:8) by which he is gifted with faith (Rom. 12:3; Eph. 2:8).

Justification and baptism—When the elect individual responds to his regeneration with faith, he is justified before God (Rom. 3:28, 5:1; Gal. 2:16, 3:11, 24; Phil. 3:9). Justification is an act of the Holy Spirit (1 Cor. 6:11) in which the forensic righteousness of Jesus Christ is imputed to the new believer. Recall that Jesus Christ fulfilled the law through his perfect obedience under the law in both his life and death. It is this forensic righteousness that is imputed to the new believer. Being justified, the elect individual no longer faces condemnation (Rom. 8:1). He is no longer under the law because he has died to it (Rom. 7.4, 6). Since his federal head, Jesus Christ, died to fulfill the law, the elect individual also died with him (Rom. 6:6, 8; Col. 2:20; Col. 3:3) and died to the law. The elect are no longer under the law; they are under grace (Rom. 6:14). Dying with Christ is being baptism into Christ's death (Rom. 6:3). It is the only baptism that saves and is referred to whenever someone is told that they must be baptized to be saved (Acts 2:38, 11:16; Gal. 3:27). In addition, this spiritual baptism includes rising with Christ to a new life (Rom. 6:4; Eph. 2:6).

Understanding Christ's federal headship—The names of the elect were recorded in The Lamb's Book of Life before creation (Phil. 4:3; Rev. 3:5, 21:22-27). The elect were chosen and predestined in love by the Father before creation (Eph. 1:4-5). These took place before time and challenge us to conceptualize what "before" means in this pretemporal context. Paul writes that the saints have been (past tense) predestined, called, justified, and even glorified just as if all has already happened (Rom. 8:30). Some events recorded in Scripture are fixed in time, such as Jesus was born (Matt. 1:16, 2:1), Christ died once (Heb. 7:27) and rose from the grave in three days (Luke 24:46; John 21:14; 1 Pet. 1:3, 21). These are physical events fixed in time but designed and superintended with divine power and grace.

Likewise, though invisible to us, our quilt was imputed to Christ by divine power. It is described as our sin having been nailed to the cross (Col. 2:14), which includes sins we have not yet committed. We were not present at these events, yet we died and were buried with Christ (Rom. 6:4, 8; Col. 2:20, 3:3) and later rose with him (Col. 3:1). This can only be resolved by noting that Jesus Christ is our federal head and what he did in his flesh was as if we had done it in our flesh. As in Adam's sin, we all sinned, so the elect are made righteous in Christ's righteousness. It is as if the Holy Spirit provides the new believer with a death certificate signed in Christ's blood and a new birth certificate sealed with divine grace and power. Of course, no such certificates are given, but the forensic righteousness of Christ is imputed to the new believer, and God is at peace with him.

Christ the Redeemer, the Propitiator—Because Christ, as a qualified kinsman redeemer, paid the debt of sin that we owed, he has ransomed us from the debt we owed to the Father (Matt. 20:28; Col. 2:14; 1 Pet. 1:18; 1 Ti. 2:6) and thus the elect have been redeemed through Jesus Christ (Rom. 3:24; 1 Cor. 1:30; Eph. 1:30; Col. 1:14; Heb. 9:12). Having redeemed the elect, Christ is properly called our Redeemer (Gal. 3:13; Rev. 14:3-4) and so we belong to him (1 Cir. 15:23; Gal. 5:24; Titus 2:14; 1 Pet. 2:9).

Related to redemption and justification is propitiation. The elect are justified and propitiated by Christ, who shed his blood for our sins (Rom 3:25, 5:9; 1 John 2:2, 4:10). Redemption involves settling a debt. Justification involves a legal declaration of being righteous. Propitiation delivers the elect from God's wrath (1 Thess. 1:10, 5:9) and establishes peace between the elect and God (Rom. 5:1; Col. 1:20; 2 Pet. 3:14). When a new believer comes in faith, they are justified and at peace with God (Rom. 5:1, 3:25).

The role of faith—Justification is a free gift of grace (Rom 3:25). When an elect individual comes to faith, God declares him legally justified and righteous. Being "justified by faith," as expressed in Romans 3:28 and 5:1, means that the believer has been declared justified as a legal verdict. But the righteousness that justification depends on is a free gift of grace, not faith. So, faith does not make a person justified. God is the justifier, and counts one is justified when they have faith in Jesus (Rom. 3:26). When Adam sinned, we all sinned in Adam (Rom. 5:12). We had to come into the world for Adam's sin to be accounted to us. Likewise, we had to be born again and believe in Jesus for Christ's righteousness to be accounted to us. Faith has no part in being born again or regeneration; it is all of grace. Faith is instrumental in justification and further sanctification and is never causative. Justification may also be understood to mean that the elect, having been born again, are justified, but their justification is only manifested through faith.

By God's design—All that occurs to bring an individual into the kingdom of Christ is according to the Father's design, decretive will, and divine power (2 Peter 1:3-5). No part of coming to Christ depends on the individual. God's plan for the Son to bear the sins of the elect, all that was necessary in preparation for that to be possible and effectual, and what benefits it bestows upon the elect, as it unfolds in history, is a story of divine love (1 John 4:10).

Christ's death on the cross—There are several critical theological facts believers should understand about Jesus' death on the cross.

1. According to Scripture (1 Cor. 15:3; Gen. 3:15; Ps. 22; Isa. 53:1-12; Dan 9:24-26; Zech. 13:7), Paul received the central issue of the Gospel, that Christ died for our

sins, which he delivered unchanged. Notably, Paul pointed out that this was not a secondary plan of God.

2. Jesus Christ bore our sins and thus freed us from the bondage of sin and delivered us from the present evil age (Rom. 8:21; Gal. 1:4). There is more to consider about being saved than going to heaven rather than hell when we die. A dramatic change has occurred in the saints' lives, having been born again. They have escaped the corruption of the world, both having been part of it and the judgment that is due it (2 Pet. 1:4). Thus, how the saints live is altogether changed, and they are now able to please God (Rom 8:8; Heb. 11:6).

3. The Father planned Jesus' death from eternity past (Gal. 1:4; Acts 2:23; 1 John 4:10).

4. The atonement brought about by Christ's crucifixion was entirely effectual for those for whom he died. All those chosen by God and predestined for adoption as sons through Jesus Christ (Eph. 1:4-5) will come to glory because of the efficacy of Christ's atonement (Rom. 8:30). The efficacy of the cross is by grace alone (Eph. 2:5, 8). Christ's death on the cross did not make grace available, nor was it given in part or universally. Those not among the elect receive nothing related to salvation from Christ's crucifixion (Rom. 11:7; Matt. 7:23; 1 Cor. 1:18).

Because of our former nature inherited from Adam, we were slaves to sin and were owed the wages of death, not only spiritual death but eternal death. Set against that is God's free gift of eternal life in Jesus Christ, who is our Lord (Rom. 6:23). This is not referring to some gift that has to be opened to receive fully; it is not an invitation to come to Christ. John 3:16 is a declaration, not an invitation or an offer. You need not be a Jew descended from Abraham to be among the elect, as Jesus told Nicodemus; you must be born again (John 3).

The Father planned the circumstances of Jesus' death because he loved us. Furthermore, Christ gave himself to this plan willingly. How was God's love manifested to us? God's salvific love that elects, predestines, calls, justifies, and glorifies individuals is particular to specific individuals according to the Father's will (Eph. 1:5,9,11). This love does not encompass the whole of humanity.

By his wounds, you have been healed

The prophet Isaiah foresaw the suffering servant many centuries earlier and wrote that he [Jesus] bore our griefs and carried our sorrows. He brought us peace by his chastisement, and we were healed by his wounds (Isa. 53:4). The wounds Isaiah referred to were according to God's definite plan (Acts 2:23) and consisted of the violent way the Jews mistreated him, the scourging he received by the Romans, the wounds he received while carrying his cross to Golgotha, the wounds he received when and while he was crucified, and his death for these wounds became lethal. What Hebrew, when reading 1 Peter 2:24, would not reflect on these verses and others that were written long before by Isaiah?

There are two things Peter is drawing our minds to. The first is to bring us to this truth that throughout history, there has been one faith, one means of salvation, one savior, and one eternal plan of God. He is not concocting a new theology, a new mode of salvation, or a new religion. By quoting Isaiah, he establishes that the covenant of grace has always been the overarching covenant between God and man for salvation. Secondly, Isaiah wrote of a servant to come and who would suffer. We now look upon Jesus, who has come, been manifested, and accomplished all that the prophets wrote of him. Yes, we have been healed by his wounds, but it is paramount to realize that these wounds were upon the Son of God. No other person's wounds could suffice to heal against sin and inequity but his and his alone. And by Christ's wounds, we are healed, not in part, not for a season, but entirely and for eternity. The scope of his suffering may come into focus as we reflect on Isaiah's passage. Christ's humiliation alone could not satisfy divine judgment against sin. The Roman scourging that Christ received could not satisfy divine judgment against sin. The chastisement that Isaiah wrote of was the full measure of divine judgment against sin that required a blood sacrifice, his death, and all his wounds and suffering. By that and nothing less, we are healed.

For you were straying like sheep

Although Peter's audience may have thought of themselves as being among God's chosen people, the circumstances of their lives were very much like that of lost sheep being scattered across Asia Minor and living among Gentiles. Their spiritual home had always been with God. He had always guided and guarded them, but now, instead of seeing him from afar through types and shadows, they see him as the person of Jesus Christ. The metaphor has already been established that Jesus is the good shepherd who lays down his life for his sheep (John 10:11). There is an intimacy in this relationship as each knows the other (John 10:14), which is to say, lovingly.

It is essential to be among Christ's sheep since those who aren't do not believe (John 10:26). In contrast, those who are among Christ's sheep are given eternal life so that they will never perish (John 10:27). By implication, those not among Christ's sheep will eventually perish in unbelief. Continuing the metaphor, Jesus explains further that it is the Father who gives Christ his sheep and that they are securely in his and the Father's hands (John 10:28-29).

Peter continues drawing us to Isaiah 53 in verse 6. Isaiah could only envision the coming of the suffering servant, but he has been made manifest to us. Isaiah saw that Christ's suffering would bring us peace with God as our iniquity was laid upon him even though we have each turned to our own ways. But with more clarity, Peter explains that this is done by returning to the Shepherd and Overseer of our souls. Therein, he uses the metaphor to include Jesus as the Overseer of our souls, a title that brings us to the realization that we are not the stewards of ourselves. That responsibility belongs solely to Jesus as the apostle and high priest sent by God, who is faithful over God's house, the communion of saints, as a son (Heb. 3:1-6), and who will guard us in body and soul through to glory as he has declared (John 6:44).

This is the goodness of Christ we have each tasted, as mentioned in verse 3. Christ is good to us, not because we have come to him but because, by taking our chastisement upon himself, he is the way for us to go to the Father (John 14:6). There is much to understand from this. The church is God's property, purchased at the high cost of Christ's blood. The Holy Spirit has appointed overseers to care for his church. To honor Christ in this appointment, overseers must pay attention to themselves and the flock so that neither wanders from the truth or godly living (Acts 20:28). But Peter is writing about the Overseer of our very souls, the Lord Jesus Christ who shed his blood to save sinners (1 Tim. 1:15).

Chapter 2 Summary

In Chapter 1, Peter laid the foundation for understanding what we experience as Christians in a fallen world and the trials and sufferings we endure. Our experiences are part of God's plan according to his purposes, which he guards us through by his power. Although we may suffer now, an inexpressible joy awaits us, which the Father has secured. Faith is the instrument through which the Father graciously guards our souls, and we are reminded and given much evidence of the necessity of being obedient children. This vindication of God's holiness and righteousness as we suffer under various trials is a theodicy.

As we begin reading the first words of Chapter 2, we are reminded of Chapter 1 and exhorted to put off the things of our former lives. But now it is important to consider Peter's perspective about those to whom he is writing. He is writing to believers dispersed throughout Galatia living within a pagan culture. But his instruction is eternal and as relevant today as it was in his time. He is writing to people who have a sense of being aliens in a foreign land, a people without a nation, and who lack a unifying identity. Indeed, we have all come to Christ, but we have come as individuals. But in Chapter 2, Peter is expanding our perspective on what we have come to. He is giving us a new vision of ourselves and our faith. In this chapter, we see that God has not abandoned us but has brought us together, forming us corporately and collectively into a spiritual house, making us a holy and royal priesthood and a holy nation. Although we do not possess a land of our own, we are God's chosen possession. This should be understood as a single possession—the church as a single body. This is as true today as it was then and will always be. Chapter 2 encourages us to understand better who and what we have become. By being drawn by the Father to Christ, we have been spiritually drawn together into a family, a household, and a nation. Offering spiritual sacrifices unto God as a holy and royal priesthood has become our collective identity and service. We are God's chosen possession, purchased by the blood and obedience of his Son, our Shepherd and Overseer.

> So then you are no longer strangers and aliens, but you are fellow citizens with the saints and members of the household of God, built on the foundation of the apostles and prophets, Christ Jesus himself being the cornerstone, in whom the whole structure, being joined together, grows into a holy temple in the Lord. In him you also are being built together into a dwelling place for God by the Spirit. (Eph. 2:19-22 ESV)

Some people profess that by believing in Christ, they are members of his church even though they have not formally joined a church and neither attended nor participated in one. Is what they profess consistent with what Peter describes as belonging to the church of Jesus Christ? Are they visibly part of anything that looks like a spiritual household? Do they offer spiritual sacrifices as visible participants in a holy priesthood? Are they connected in any visible way to the body of believers unified as a spiritual nation? Indeed, the answer to such inquiries is "no." This does not imply they are not true believers but have the wrong understanding and vision of what it means to have come to Jesus Christ. It is inappropriate to profess membership in the invisible church while repudiating membership in its visible aspect. The church's attributes enumerated by apostles Peter and Paul are realized in both aspects of the church as it is to the visible church the apostles have written. A memorable passage from Chapter 2:

But you are a chosen race, a royal priesthood, a holy nation, a people for his own possession, that you may proclaim the excellencies of him who called you out of darkness into his marvelous light. Once you were not a people, but now you are God's people; once you had not received mercy, but now you have received mercy. (1 Pet. 2:9-10 ESV).

Chapter 3 – When We Suffer

Introduction

Peter continues with doctrinal applications for Christian living by focusing on relationships, which he had begun in Chapter 2, having exhorted believers to be obedient to the civil government and servants to their masters. His exhortation to all of us is to be submissive to whatever authority is over us in all fear of God, for God has called us to our circumstances, and he will guard us through them. These exhortations continue in Chapter 3 and are a principal focus of the chapter.

Peter addresses wives, spending six verses explaining the appropriate conduct of wives and the benefits of godly conduct. Only a single verse addresses the conduct of husbands, but this brevity is due to avoid repetition. Following these specific relationships, Peter's exhortations turn to the general nature of Christian living, where he spends ten verses. The final five verses of Chapter 3 return to doctrine, where we encounter some difficulty with Peter's awkward writing style.

Several verses stand out with particular importance. Of wives, may it be verse 4, *"but let your adorning be the hidden person of the heart with the imperishable beauty of a gentle and quiet spirit, which in God's sight is very precious"* (ESV). With Christian living, I suggest it is the phrase in verse 15, *"always being prepared to make a defense to anyone who asks you for a reason for the hope that is in you*" (ESV). And of Peter's Christology, I would say verses 18 and 22, "*For Christ also suffered once for sins, the righteous for the unrighteous, that he might bring us to God, being put to death in the flesh but made alive in the spirit,*" and "*who has gone into heaven and is at the right hand of God, with angels, authorities, and powers having been subjected to him*" (ESV).

3:1-8 Relationships Within the Church: Wives and Husbands

There is much of Chapters 1 and 2 on which Chapter 3 rests. Peter has drawn a spiritual panorama of the church in Chapter 2 that is majestic and glorious. Should we examine it up close and see its very elements, we find each is a believer called to Christ, brought to the Father, and guarded through faith. As members of this spiritual household, Peter has been exhorting us how we should live, with all respect and fear for our heavenly Father, in executing his eternal plan and bringing all things to their proper and necessary end according to the purpose of his will. Based on that, Peter continues to instruct wives and husbands in these relationships, our conduct within the church to one another, and our response to those who in some way cause us to suffer by their words or actions. He ends this chapter by returning our focus to Christ, his suffering for us, and his example of obedience.

1 Peter 3:1-2

Be subject to your husband

In the framework of what Peter has already laid out for us, how we should conduct ourselves in relationships, which he began in Chapter 2, he immediately draws our minds to it with the word "Likewise" and addresses instructions to wives.

Following the Jews' return from exile to Galatia, they began intermarrying with Gentiles. In these mixed marriages, believing wives found themselves married to nonbelieving husbands and vice versa. Nevertheless, there is an established order of authority within the marital relationship. The husband is the head of the relationship (1 Cor. 7:13) even if he is a nonbeliever, and a wife is not free from her responsibility to be subject to his authority over her (Eph. 5:22-24; Col. 3:18) and should not think she is free from this duty or from the marriage itself.

In the passages referred to by Paul, he explains why a wife should submit to her husband, whereas Peter, in his usual brevity, states it as an imperative, "*be subject.*" But then Peter adds words of encouragement for believing wives who may be married to nonbelieving husbands. By your good conduct, a nonbelieving husband might be won over to the Lord when he sees "*your respectful and pure conduct.*"

Such conduct is a Christian witness, for in the case of a nonbelieving husband, such godly conduct puts forth an example of goodness, respect, and pure conduct that cannot be denied. By inference, Peter is disclosing that the Holy Spirit may use the witness of a godly wife to bring her nonbelieving husband to Christ, as does Paul (1 Cor. 7:16).

1 Peter 3:3

Do not let your adorning be external

Peter's list of external adornments is to be taken seriously. However, it should not be concluded that the apostle forbids all braids, jewelry, or specific garments. Such things should be judged according to the times and cultures and within reasonable bounds. However, the principle that wives are to be subject to their husbands, which Peter is exhorting wives to follow, is a matter of God's unchanging and authoritative word.

We should understand Peter's list of external adornments in the following way. Generally speaking, men tend to imagine more than their eyes see. Women should consider this regarding their appearance to avoid being sensual and immoderate. Both men and women should understand that the respectful and gentle nature of the heart, which is precious to God, should also be precious to us. How we present ourselves in our speech, actions, and appearance should always express our Christian profession.

1 Peter 3:4

The hidden person of the heart

The principle of verses 3 and 4 is that there is an inner and precious beauty, particularly in women, which can be seen and that God adores. This beauty lies in the inner person possessing a gentle and quiet nature. Until a woman's conduct reveals it, it remains hidden, unlike any external adornments. As this inner beauty does not fade with age, it is imperishable. When a wife is subject to her husband with a quiet and gentle nature, she is pleasing to God, who sees her inner person as beautiful and precious.

More and more these days, we see women being ordained as deacons, elders, and pastors. Behind much of this, if not entirely, is Bible Feminism. Bible Feminism purports that Paul and Peter wrote from their patriarchal backgrounds and also Paul from his rabbinical background. In other words, they were not writing under the inspiration of the Holy Spirit. Thus, whatever does not appeal to Bible Feminists in Scripture, they assign to the alleged biases and prejudices of the apostles. This would mean that the Bible is a "living document" and subject to being reinterpreted as human culture progresses. This is precisely what Bible Feminists claim is hermeneutical but is appropriately called *cultural relativism*. Accordingly, not only is Peter's list of examples of external adornments repudiated, but also the entire exhortation of verse 1. There is a regressive weakening of Chapter 2 since Chapter 3 explicitly states that wives are to be subject to their husbands based on the application of Chapter 2.

1 Peter 3:5-6

Like the holy women

Peter reinforces this exhortation with an example. Women who adorned themselves from within did so by submitting to the will of God and being subject to their husbands. They did so because their hope was in God. God is now pleased to count them as holy women. Among these holy women is Sarah, and the women who follow her are the ones God is pleased to call her children. Peter knows this is difficult and reminds wives not to be afraid to do good even during times of difficulty.

1 Peter 3:7

Likewise, husbands show honor

What Peter has written to wives concerning the general principles of godly respect and subjection to their husbands, we may now infer equally applies to husbands towards their wives. He continues with the special duties a husband owes his wife. To live with your wife is to live in a marital relationship, performing all its duties and responsibilities. This is particularly applicable should a man's wife not be a believer. In that case, he should continue to be her husband and not seek a divorce. Specifically, the husband is to perform his duties as a husband in a manner that demonstrates the honor due to his wife. His instructions to husbands benefit both husbands and wives when husbands submit from the heart to live according to their calling as husbands.

Show honor

We will return to the phrase "*as the weaker vessel*," following comments on the rest of the verse. There are reasons why a husband must show honor to his wife. The first is that they are co-heirs of the grace of life. Harshness ensues in the absence of honor and love, so husbands are elsewhere exhorted not to be harsh (Col. 3:19).

As a man has the duty to help the poor, so does a husband have the duty to honor his wife. According to Proverbs 14:31, the one who oppresses the poor fails on three counts. (1) He does not fulfill his duties to show mercy, compassion, and help in a time of need. This we infer from general principles. (2) By not performing his duty, he demonstrates that he does not esteem the poor worthy of such respect. This is an insult to God, who is their Maker. (3) In the same manner, a husband who does not honor his wife fails in this duty, does not properly esteem or respect his wife, and insults God, who has brought them together and established them in marriage.

The honor owed to one's wife stems partly from her being an heir to the grace of life. She is due this honor in Christ, and the husband has no right to withhold it from her. It is as much his duty in Christ to show honor to his wife as it is her right in Christ to receive it. A Christian husband who does not show honor to his wife demonstrates his lack of esteem for her, for her right to it, and for Christ whose grace they have each received.

A husband must honor his wife to maintain a good conscience before the Lord. Otherwise, he is engaged in wrongdoing and may become disinclined to pray before the Lord. His anxiety may mute his prayers, which may not be heard (Prov. 15:29).

As the weaker vessel

We have seen why a husband should honor his wife. It is imperative to understand that the husband and wife are co-equals as they are co-heirs of the grace of life. Being weaker does not mean or imply inferiority. Since the wife is noted as the weaker vessel, both husband and wife are considered vessels in some way. The Bible uses terms like "*vessel*" to refer to people in several places. In Acts 9:15, Paul is referred to as a chosen instrument. In 2 Corinthians 4:7, jars of clay describe the vessels which contain our understanding of the knowledge of the glory of God. In 2 Timothy 2:21, individuals are called vessels to be used. Paul, when teaching about election, referred to people as vessels of wrath (Rom. 9:22) and vessels of mercy (Rom. 9:23). As we consider what vessels mean in a Biblical sense, it falls out that they are the design of God to be used for his purposes. Thus, in the context of 1 Peter 3:7, the husband is reminded that he is also a vessel, accountable to God, and that the honor he owes to his wife must take into account that she is somehow, of the two, a weaker vessel. How a husband honors his wife must consider whether the wife is being built up and strengthened. If she is not, then her husband is not fulfilling his duty to honor her appropriately. Peter draws the husbands' attention to their wives' designed relative weakness, which must be considered when honoring them as dutiful husbands.

So that your prayers may not be hindered

Later in this epistle, Peter will warn us again about our prayers. We can infer that our prayers may be adversely affected if we do not keep our actions and thoughts in line with good conduct and a good conscience (Pro. 15:29; 1 Pet. 4:7). We may, for a time, withdraw from prayer or from praying whole heartily, the Lord my turn his hearing away, and we may even grieve the Holy Spirit (Eph. 4:30; 1 Pet. 3:12). In the context of verse 7, Peter is indeed making us aware that the proper duties a husband owes his wife are of such importance, that the failure to perform them with lovingkindness from the heart is such an occasion that our prayers might not come forth or be heard (Isa. 59:1-2). We read elsewhere in Scripture an exhortation to have a pure heart (2 Tim. 2:22) by which we may call upon the Lord. To have a pure heart, a husband must love his wife and fulfill his duties to her joyfully.

Marriage in the pagan world

Since Peter has addressed the marital relation with instructions to wives and husbands, we can infer that the marriage relation, as defined in Scripture, is exclusively between one man and one woman who become husband and wife when joined in marriage. Let us not be misled or deceived by what is embraced and celebrated in the pagan world as marriage or become passively reconciled to abominations of this holy institution within the church (Gen. 2:24; Pro. 2:17; Matt. 19:5, 6; Mal 2:15; 1 Cor. 7:2, 9; WCF 24.1, 2; LBC 25. 1, 2).

1 Peter 3:8

Peter begins by informing us that this is his final section on relationships within the church and conduct among the saints. These exhortations are directed to the church as a body but must be fulfilled by each member for the sake of the whole. They are intended to lead each church member into the proper relationship of mind and heart within the family of God so that there may be peace and unity among the believers. In what Peter writes, he excludes no one. Whether you have just entered the church from the pagan world, are a member of long-standing, or are a leader and shepherd, these exhortations apply to you. As we explore these exhortations individually, we will find they are interrelated and connected.

Have unity of mind

The word *"unity"* implies there is a community being addressed. The facts we believe, the things we think, the meanings we assign to things we see and hear, and the plans we make are all functions of the mind. Peter is guiding us to use our minds for the common good of the church, for God's chosen people. There should be no mavericks whose plans are for their own purposes and not the church's welfare. God knows the minds of his creatures (Ps. 7:9; Heb. 4:12), and to demonstrate the nature of our minds, he tests us in ways that reveal the spiritual leanings of our hearts and minds.

In Psalm 119, Samekh equates those who do not have regard for God's commandments and go astray of the law as double-minded. To Samekh, such double-mindedness is evil. He sees their influence as making it more difficult for him to be righteous and seeks the Lord's protection from them. Psalm 119 underscores the importance of having unity of mind among God's people and helps us understand Peter's context.

Proverbs 19 informs us that although we make many plans, only those that conform to God's purpose come to fruition (verse 21). As we mature, we learn to think with the mind of Christ more and more. The mind of Christ is the ability of a regenerate mind to think in the manner of Christ, and as believers strive for this mind of Christ, they will naturally have unity of mind (1 Cor. 2:16).

Both Peter and Paul (Phil. 1:27) exhort us to be of one mind. They do not mean we must always think alike, order the same meals at restaurants, and like the same flavor of ice cream. Instead, we should be of one mind so that all our efforts for the sake of the faith and the gospel are aligned so that our striving is not at cross-purposes. Being of one mind is so important to Paul as an essential characteristic of any congregation and the church that he repeats this exhortation in the same letter (Phil. 2:2).

Have sympathy

Peter's instruction is meant for believers to have sympathy for each other. When adversity strikes a believer or their family, it affects the whole body of believers. He has told us that we will endure trials and suffering and that God will guard and protect us. Our faith is at the heart of this as an instrument of God's grace, but it is not the only instrument. There is a purpose for the church to fulfill when its members suffer. Peter is not merely exhorting believers to be sad when seeing a member in need or disadvantaged without extending whatever help and support is necessary. Instead, the sympathy we should experience toward a brother or sister in the Lord should compel us to be merciful, generous, supportive, encouraging, helpful, and prayerful.

Paul expresses this exceptionally well. In Philippians 1, he describes his own suffering and preference to depart and be with Christ but acknowledges the necessity of continuing to minister. In Philippians 2, Paul seeks comfort from the saints' love, participation in the Spirit, and their affection and sympathy, which they owe him in Christ. He presses to a higher goal than his own comfort that they are of one mind and have the same love. Paul has in mind here that the Philippians agree with the doctrines of the faith and the affections of the heart (Phil. 2:1-2).

Apostle John poses the following rhetorical question for which we immediately understand the proper answer. How does God's love abide in a man if he possesses what a brother needs but closes his heart to him (1 John 3:17)? Peter tells us that every brother and sister in the Lord should receive our sympathy when needed. John further informs us that genuine sympathy expresses God's love for our brothers and compels us to seek their welfare.

Have brotherly love

Brotherly love is a duty of the Christian life (Rom. 12:10; Heb. 13:1) that arises from the affections of a heart rooted in Christ. Whether God immediately or mediately imparts the affection we should have for our brothers and sisters in the Lord, we nevertheless must nurture love within ourselves for them (1 Thess. 4:9). The love and affection shared by believers first comes from a purified soul. Then, from a pure heart and with sincerity (1 Pet. 1:22). There are no hidden or cross-purposes allowed in such love.

If we explore Peter's writings further, into his second epistle, we find that brotherly love is counted among the qualities with which we may supplement our faith. Indeed, he exhorts us to make every effort to acquire and practice all qualities that supplement our faith for their manifold benefits (1 Pet. 1:5) and to confirm our calling and election (2 Pet. 1:10).

Have a tender heart

Being tenderhearted joins well with brotherly love and sympathy. Peter is giving us instructions for the church's welfare. By his short and simple phrase, we are instructed that the condition of the human heart is of great importance and interest to God, as it should be to us. A tender heart is filled with compassion (Col. 3:12) and is open to instruction. It is a heart that the knowledge and weight of sin have broken, is filled with remorse (Ps. 51:17), and strives to be clean (Ps. 51:10), upright (Ps. 7:10), and pure (Matt. 5:8).

In the absence of a tender heart, there is hardheartedness and even "wicked obstinacy," as John Calvin phrases it. This rightly reminds us that God knows the hearts of men, what is held in secret there, and what emanates from the heart (Ps. 44:21; Acts 15:8; Heb 4:12). God guards and works on the hearts of men to establish the righteous by testing their hearts and renewing in them a right spirit to create clean hearts (Ps. 7:9; Ps. 51:10; Phil. 4:7).

These are the qualities of a heart that is right with God:

1. a tender heart (1 Pet. 3:8)

2. a clean heart (Ps. 51:10)

3. a broken and contrite heart (Ps. 51:17)

4. a compassionate heart (Co. 3:12)

5. an upright heart (Ps. 7:10)

6. a pure heart (Matt. 5:8)

Have a humble mind

"With humility is wisdom" (Pro. 11:2) means that the wise, those who possess wisdom, know to be humble. True humility is a virtue which, as we will see, is recognized and rewarded by God. Being humble does not mean that a person must debase themself to the extent that they perceive themself to be of no value. While we recognize that we are recipients of God's grace, we also acknowledge that we have done nothing to merit it. This involves having a frame of mind about who we were, who we have become, and what God did

to make us so. This was accomplished by God's grace, not by our works (Rom. 11:6). The price God paid to ransom the elect overwhelms us (1 Pet. 1:18-19; 1 Cor. 6:20). It certainly indicates that God had deemed the elect to be of great worth to himself. But that is not to imply that the elect were themselves worthy to be so valued.

The apostles continue to exhort us to live in a worthy manner consistent with being the sons of God (Eph. 4:1). It does not mean that we have to make ourselves worthy before becoming the sons of God. It means that as the sons of God, we should live in a manner that represents and demonstrates its reality.

We are told to recognize that the saints have a certain worthiness because they are saints (Rom. 12:10, 16:2). That worthiness must inherently result from God's love, election, and grace upon them. According to Scripture, there should be no brother among us who feels they are not loved and do not feel welcome and honored.

The apostles have told us a lot about what we have become in Christ, who we are in the sight of God, what the Father has done through the Son to bring this about (2 Pet. 1:3-4), and what more he will do (Phil. 1:6). While we hold to this by faith, it is all by grace alone and not by our works. It is an unmerited gift of unimaginable worth. We came into this life as sons of Adam with the due and righteous judgment of everlasting torment hanging over us. However, we will leave this life as sons of God, having been predestined by the Father through Jesus Christ for adoption as sons (1 Pet. 1:5). The difference between those who will go into the pit of eternal fire and the elect who will reign in glory is all of grace. Every elect soul knows that they brought nothing with them into this life and have done nothing during this life for which God owes them a moment in heaven.

In all of this, we are never told or encouraged not to love ourselves (Matt. 19:19). We are never given a reason not to love ourselves. Neither have we been told to think that we are worthy or have become worthy of the grace we have received.

People may do the right thing but with the wrong motive. While having a pretense of humility is possible, Peter is concerned with the inner person. Acts of humility done only to be seen and draw attention to oneself are the products of a prideful mind. His concern is for a godly mind to oversee the faculties of the soul (Phil. 2:3-8).

Being humble requires a personal commitment that can be either accomplished or resisted. Humility can be turned on and off, but Peter exhorts believers to maintain humility as a constant state of mind. The Lord notices and blesses those who humble themselves (Matt. 18:4; Luke 14:11; Jas 4:10).

If pridefulness is the state of the mind without humility, it is worth exploring what Peter is exhorting us to avoid. Pride and a haughty spirit lead to a fall and destruction (Pro. 16:18). It is precisely this potential for destruction that Peter is exhorting the church to avoid. Imagine a church whose members lack humility, in which every member thinks of themselves as better, superior, more worthy, and more deserving than all others. Everyone would always compete with pride, jealousy, and envy erupting until no one could stand it any longer. This may be a worst-case scenario, but it establishes what Peter commands us to avoid.

3:9-12 Christian Conduct During Trials Part 1

The remaining exhortations are more general. They are intended to instruct the saints how to respond to others who afflict them. The one whom we are not to repay in kind is not specified. Many commentaries place this person in the secular and pagan world and thus explain his instruction only in the context of how Christians are to respond to non-Christians who afflict us. Perhaps we should understand that Peter teaches how Christians should react to afflictions from anyone, Christian and non-Christian. I consider this to be the case. Indeed, a fellow church member can do evil things and speak falsely against another member. If that happens, how should the offended church member respond other than according to Peter's instructions given here?

1 Peter 3:9

Called to bless

We have a calling to be extraordinarily tolerant, even when poorly treated (Matt. 5:39; Rom 12:14-21). The issue is how we respond once evil is committed against us. Our Lord has told us to lend ourselves to receive a similar blow. By this instruction, we defuse the anger and desire for revenge within ourselves, which we might take action on and are prevented from inciting further malice from the evil one.

Suppose we apply what Peter has written to the interactions that might occur among believers when things get heated or out-of-hand. Rather than incite things further and drive an argument to a higher pitch by exchanging wound for wound, Peter wants us to strive to return things to the peacefulness that should characterize brotherly love. He reminds us that we have been called to bless one another, to seek only the good for each other, and should we do so, the very peace achieved will be a blessing. On the other hand, when a nonbeliever commits evil against us, our response should be that of a good witness for Christ.

The sorts of things Peter refers to as evil and reviling include physical and verbal abuse, slander, libel, gossip, false accusations, theft, as well as other things (Ps. 7:14). Evil things done to us and reviling are more egregious when committed and initiated by believers against fellow believers. If we are exhorted not to respond in kind when such is done against us from the pagan world, it is even more imperative not to respond in kind when the perpetrator is a fellow church member (2 Cor. 12:20).

We find an extraordinary example from Paul (1 Cor. 4:9-13) about his and the other apostles' response when reviled. Under extraordinary mistreatment and hardship, the apostles maintained a faithful witness of the faith they professed. The world perceived them as human refuse and treated them as such, but they always returned blessings for reviling, entreating when slandered, and endurance when persecuted. If the apostles bless those in the world who reviled and persecuted them, it is certainly incumbent upon us to bless those who revile us, especially within the household of God.

Peter draws from Psalm 34 as he continues to entice us to good behavior with the hope of a blessing. Someone has just harmed or offended you and has made you feel angry. If you strike back and perpetuate the discord, there will only be continued strife and an absence of peace for yourself and possibly the church. If, on the other hand, you restrain yourself from responding in kind but instead bless, the argument no longer has legs to stand on, and good and happier days are sure to follow (Ps. 34:14).

1 Peter 3:10

The tongue

Psalm 34:13 says, *"Keep your tongue from evil and your lips from speaking deceit"* (ESV). The apostle James has much to tell us about the use of speech as he refers to our use of it to harm each other via the tongue. If we do not follow the psalmist's advice, James tells us we deceive ourselves to the extent that we hold to a worthless religion (Jas. 1:26). He likens the unbridled tongue to a small fire that sets a whole forest ablaze. It is an untamed and restless evil that can ruin a person's life (Jas. 3:5-10).

The evil Peter is referring to is committed by either party in an exchange, by the one who first initiates it and by the one who is provoked by it. According to him, restraining yourself from such evil comes from the heart of those who desire to love life and see good days. He implies that if you initiate or continue strife, unhappy days and a sorrowful life may follow.

1 Peter 3:11

Turn away

The commission of sin is preceded by temptation. Before the deed occurs, the thought of the deed arises. Peter is telling believers to turn away from such thoughts of evil acts so as not to commit them. He is telling both parties in an exchange to do this. The one with thoughts of committing an evil act against his brother is told to stop and restrain himself. The one provoked by such evil is also told to restrain himself so as not to do likewise. Not only turn away from doing evil but turn to doing good. John Calvin wrote that it is not enough to embrace peace when offered but to seek and pursue it. Even when salvos of insults harm us, we are exhorted not only to seek peace but to seek it with extraordinary effort, including blessing those who revile us.

1 Peter 3:12

The eyes of the Lord

Peter reminds us that our Father in heaven guards us through trials and suffering, which is to say these things are out of our hands. Should we not submit ourselves to the exhortations of his apostles and conduct ourselves rightly by always turning to the good and seeking peace, especially among God's people, our prayers will be hindered as God sets his face against us for the evil we do, whether we initiate it or return it (Pro. 15:3). Peter's instruction is of critical importance to keep in mind when injured by some malicious words or actions. If someone were to sow the seeds of discord between brothers, do not nurture further discord but let the Lord deal with the one sowing discord in God's household. It is not only the discord that God hates but also the one who sows discord among brothers (Pro. 16:16-19).

Notice in this excerpt from Psalm 16 that *"one who sows discord among brothers,"* the person himself is an abomination to the Lord. Paul warns that biting and devouring one another may lead to you being consumed (Gal. 5:15).

Paul instructed Titus about dealing with people who stir up divisions within the church through church discipline. Warn them once and even twice, but if they do not relent from discord, have nothing to do with them, which is to be taken as putting them out of the fellowship (Titus 3:10). The very next verse states that such persons are sinful and self-condemned. Indeed, the Lord knows our hearts.

From verses 9 to 11, Peter has instructions on what our immediate response to personal injury must be from whoever originates it. We must turn away from it and not return evil for evil. However, the Lord does not leave us with this as our only response if we are sinned against by a church member. Matthew 18:5-17 deals with brother sinning against brother and establishes a process for reconciliation. If, in the end, the offending brother refuses to listen even to the church, he may then be considered an outsider. This would mean a broken fellowship and separation so that no further opportunities for sinning between these brothers might occur. Also, note that these instructions are to be conducted privately to maintain reputations, peace, and the church's welfare. Most churches have established rules for conducting formal church discipline, which should always begin by following Matthew 18 and Galatians 6:1.

3:13-17 Christian Conduct During Trials Part 2

Peter realizes that no matter how much we endeavor to avoid trouble, we may find ourselves in the mists of it. What should we then do? What course of action can we take? Peter elevates our minds in these circumstances to realize there is a difference between the harm we feel in this life and the harm that can be inflicted spiritually.

Peter 3:13

Who is there to harm you?

The interlinear Greek text begins verse 13 with "*And*" instead of "*Now*." The King James Bible also begins verse 13 with "*And*." The Greek word, kaì, from which this is translated, is used to make a connection or for emphasis. In this case, it appears that verse 12 is connected to verse 13 and what Peter has written leading up to it, so that he, in verse 13, having brought our attention to how we are regarded in the sight of God, poses a question based on the proposition that you are zealous for doing good. Peter asks, "Who is there to harm you?" Consider what happens if we return evil for evil. Do we not do more harm to ourselves than the one who first committed evil against us? Indeed, we do. If, on the other hand, we suffer when we are zealous for doing good, there is no real harm done to us in the spiritual sense. This is what Peter wants us to consider. The psalmist writes that whoever has the fear of the Lord rests satisfied, knowing that it leads to life, and thus, they will not be harmed in a spiritual sense (Ps. 19:23).

1 Peter 3:14

Suffering for righteousness' sake

Peter refers to the kind of suffering intentionally inflicted by others, not the hardships and losses we might experience otherwise. In verse 9, he told us we might obtain a blessing by not repaying evil for evil. Now, in verse 14, he promises a blessing. What has changed in the development of the text to prompt this? Verse 9 specifies certain actions to avoid and actions to take, all of which are duties we are called to perform, and when we have done them, we have only done what we have been called to do. Peter instructed us to respond in a righteous and Christ-honoring way to evil acts committed against us. This may not be able to assuage the attacks committed against us by some, but if we persist by responding righteously, we suffer for righteousness' sake, and a blessing is promised.

Have no fear

Peter considers the severe hardship one experiences when one suffers for righteousness' sake and tells us not to be overtaken with fear so that we may persist in honoring Christ with an untroubled mind and a good conscience. Rather than telling us not to fear, Paul tells us to stand firm in the faith and to be strong, to act like men (1 Cor. 16:13). Together, Peter and Paul mean our guidance in these circumstances must be from the word of God for action and encouragement and not to act rashly.

1 Peter 3:15

Honor Christ the Lord as holy

The ESV translation should have rendered ἁγιάσατε (hagiasate) as *sanctify* rather than honor (biblehub.com). Christ himself does not need to be sanctified, and Peter does not suggest any such thing. Peter refers to our hearts being sanctified by the presence of Christ and reminds us of his holiness. This is by far more profound than honoring Christ as it manifestly means a change taking place in our hearts, a change that we are actively called to engage in as it is a process of ongoing or progressive sanctification. No person can honor Christ from their heart if his indwelling presence does not first sanctify it.

Peter knows the trouble and sufferings believers can precipitate when they act unwisely and how that affects the faith. So that we may be directed to give a good and proper witness for the faith and not suffer foolishly, we must keep the focus of our hearts on the holiness of Christ and his Lordship so no matter how provoked others may make us, what we do honors him, his lordship, and his holiness. It is also true that anyone whose heart is sanctified by Christ will be less likely to revile, slander, or be evil towards a brother or neighbor.

Always be prepared

"Always be prepared" requires being informed, knowledgeable, and ready. Being prepared requires serious study and seeking true wisdom so that when we speak in defense of our hope, we may be taken seriously. Being prepared has a caveat attached. The witness Peter is exhorting us to make is in response to being asked. Certainly, we can take opportunities to witness the Gospel of Jesus Christ to others. Still, Peter is telling us that when people ask us to explain our hope, we should be all the more ready and able to explain to them as their asking may be the prompting work of the Holy Spirit.

The hope that is in you

Peter has compacted a great deal into this verse. We should ask why someone might ask us about our hope. What would prompt them to ask such a question? Certainly, it could be the Holy Spirit, and it may well be. Still, if we conduct ourselves in a Christ-honoring way, it will become apparent that our language, speech, and interactions are different from others. When we honor Christ as Lord and holy, we are best fit to be witnesses for him, first by example and then by testimony.

Peter does not write, "your hope." Instead, he writes "the hope" and points out that this hope is "in you." Peter is not writing about a fuzzy feeling that has welled up within you, a sort of desire that you would like to come true and be realized. Everyone has experienced hope of some kind at diverse times and for sundry things. Christian hope, like the Christian faith, is altogether unique.

Paul informs us that anyone without Christ has no hope (Eph. 2:12); there is no hope in or for them. This does not mean that there is nothing they can hope for or are incapable of being hopeful, but being without God renders them in a hopeless position of condemnation from which they cannot free themselves. But Paul is writing this to and about people no longer in a state of condemnation. How did their hopeless condition change? The answer is in the next verse in Ephesians, that the hope we have as saints is in the blood of Christ and all that accrues to us through it (Eph. 2:13). Without Christ, without God in the world, nothing could make a difference, and there was nothing to hope for or to place one's hope in for anything that would endure. The apostle tells us that without Christ, you have no hope. But praise God, for by the blood of Christ, you were brought near so that you are no longer without hope.

In Peter's context and compact writing style, he informs us that if we honor Christ in our hearts by conducting ourselves in a holy manner, we are people with inward hope, unlike when we were without Christ and hopeless.

What makes the Christian hope unique? If we examine verses about Christian hope, we see it is in God, in Christ, by grace and our calling, by the power of the Holy Spirit, for salvation and eternal life. Not only is Christian hope unique, but all the saints possess it as it is integral to our being called to one body and one spirit (Eph. 4:4). Hebrews Chapter 3:13-20 draws out the uniqueness of the Christian hope profoundly and gloriously. The graciousness of God is manifested in the manifold way he cares and provides for his people. Our patience as weak men and women tends to wear thin over time. As we wait as heirs of the promise, our impatient hearts convincingly need assurance and encouragement, which only God provides. He provides this by his unchangeable purpose, which he guaranteed with an oath. Since it is not possible for God to lie, we have a firm conviction to patiently hold onto the hope set before us through Jesus Christ, our hope, refuge, and high priest who has entered the holy place by his own blood as our redeemer and firstborn of many brothers (Rom. 8:29). The passage in Hebrews denotes, as a mark of God's love, that God desired to do this for our assurance of hope. God has given his people the means to remain steadfast in the hope to which we have been called, provided we keep their minds on God's purpose and Jesus Christ.

Now faith is the assurance of things hoped for, the conviction of things not seen. (Heb. 11:1 ESV)

Christian hope lies at the foundation of Christian faith as a sure and steadfast anchor of the soul that enters into the inner place behind the curtain, which is the very presence of God. Thus, Paul wrote to the Colossian Gentiles that their faith in Christ Jesus and their love for all the saints was due to the hope laid up for them in heaven (Col. 1:4-5). It is this specific hope that Peter draws our attention to by referring to it as "*the hope*" and says it is "*in you*" and which you are to give a defense for when asked.

Defense

The Greek word translated as *a defense* means to give a verbal legal argument, not just a reason. Stephen used this word in Acts 22:1 when he spoke to those who would soon stone him. In Acts 25:13-16, Festus refers to Roman law on behalf of Paul regarding Paul's right to a defense against his Jewish accusers. Paul uses this word to justify his right to work even though he was an apostle. This word for defense is used in 2 Corinthians 7 as Paul writes to the Corinthians that their godly grief brought them to repentance and to clear themselves and establish their innocence. In Philippians 1:7 and again in 1:17, Paul writes of making a defense of the gospel. In 1 Timothy 4:16, Paul refers to his first defense in Rome. All in all, the word ἀπολογίαν (apologian) is akin to a defense in a court of law.

1 Peter 3:16

Having a good conscience vs being put to shame

Peter writes under the assumption that we will respond in a Christ-honoring manner when confronted with evil against us. Therefore, we will have a good conscience. Indeed, we may only possess a truly good conscience if our conduct honors Christ. Although we may continue to suffer, those who slander and revile us or commit other evils against us because of our righteous behavior will be put to shame because they persecute the Lord through us. The Lord spoke directly to Saul while Saul was on a mission to persecute the church, asking him, *"Why are you persecuting me?"* (Acts 26:14). Christ expressed his solidarity quite clearly with those who suffer because of the neglect of others; their neglect being emblematic of an unregenerate nature. He said to them, *"Truly, I say to you, as you did not do it to one of the least of these, you did not do it to me"* (Matt. 25:45 ESV). So, from such a strong argument of Christ's solidarity with the weak and needy, we can be certain that those who trouble the church or persecute the saints, his precious possession, will be put to shame.

1 Peter 3:17

If that should be God's will

If a person were to suffer, we can be certain that their suffering would be according to God's will. A person may suffer for doing good or for doing evil, but in either case, it would be according to God's will, and Peter is not inviting us to question the sovereignty of God in our suffering. He intends to illustrate that if it is God's will that we suffer, it is better that we suffer for doing good than for doing evil.

Peter has been exhorting us about our reaction to things committed against us of an evil nature. By drawing our attention to the will of God, our thoughts become grounded in who we are dealing with and who will manage the outcome. We know because we have been told that the outcome of all things will be for our eternal good, even through difficult times (Rom. 8:28).

Therefore, we may have all the more confidence that if we return a blessing when reviled, if we honor Christ when slandered, if we present a good account of our hope when vigorously questioned, if we do not return evil for evil it will be better for us for having suffered according to God's will for doing good than if we had done or do evil instead.

3:18-22 The Foundation for Our Conduct

Good practice is established by good doctrine. Chapters 1 and 2 established a doctrinal foundation for Peter's instructions in Chapter 3, primarily on relationships and personal conduct within the church. Peter here presents the perfect example of humility, submission, and suffering for righteousness that we should, from our hearts, strive to emulate as we put into practice his instructions. His exhortations in Chapter 3 are imperative. Verses 18 through 22 eliminate any contrary thought.

Verses 13 through 17 precisely describe what Peter has exhorted us to do, even from the heart. He has written in a sort of reverse order. Often, we encounter a doctrinal statement followed by "therefore," leading us to the practice of what should follow based on the doctrine. Instead, he here has given us the practice first and follows it with its doctrinal reason. The word *"for"* in verse 18 connects the practice and the doctrine.

1 Peter 3:18.

For Christ also suffered

The word *"also"* in 1 Pet. 3:18 implies inclusion, one with another. In some manner, there is a link or connection between the suffering experienced by Christians and the suffering of Christ. Peter has this in mind: it is only natural that Christians suffer because Christ suffered. While this is true, Christ did not suffer because we suffer. But Peter elaborates on the purpose of Christ's suffering. The righteous, that is, Christ, suffered for the unrighteous, that is us. Why should the righteous one suffer for the unrighteous? Peter discloses that it was to bring us to God by being put to death and rising again. Christ's suffering was both necessary to bring us to God and completely voluntary, as God is most free. What we are led to is the gracious solidarity Christ has with us on a personal level.

Specifically, because Christ suffered on our behalf, Peter's conclusion, as should be ours, is that we can have confidence that Jesus, our high priest, will be merciful and gracious to us when we draw near to him for help (Heb. 4:14-16) so that we may suffer on his behalf.

Once for sin

As we explore this verse, we find that Peter is focused on Christ's suffering of death and its purpose. It was for sin (1 Cor. 15:3; Gal. 1:4; Heb. 1:3, 2:17), and although he includes several important details, he leaves out some that can be exposited from other verses of Scripture. The one who suffered for sin, Christ, is called *"the righteous,"* and those whose sin it was are called *"the unrighteous."* The one who did not sin (Heb. 4:15) died for the sins of others (Rom. 5:8). Christ didn't just die; he was *put to death*, meaning that his death was a judgment against sin, a judicial act of divine wrath against sin. But if Jesus did not commit sin and was innocent, how was his death justified? The guilt of the elect's sin, the whole body and mass of it, was imputed to Christ, making him guilty before God and subject to the due penalty of sin, which is death (2 Cor. 5:21).

Christ was put to death *in the flesh* (Phil. 2:6-8; 1 Tim. 3:16; 1 Pet. 4:1). Two important facts are disclosed by this. The Son of God was made incarnate as man in the flesh (John 1:14), and both his suffering and death were physically real, which we can identify with. Although Christ suffered many times throughout his earthly ministry (Heb. 2:18, 5:8, 13:12), and particularly at the hands of lawless men (Acts 2:23), he suffered only *once* for sin (Heb. 9:25-26, 10:12).

The Roman Catholic practice of the Mass, which in Protestant churches is called the Lord's Supper, deserves mentioning in light of verse 18. A common conception of the Mass is that Christ is sacrificed anew with each observance of the Mass. Another concept of the Mass is that Christ continues to suffer for the expiation of sin. 1 Peter 3:18 says, *"Christ also suffered once for sin."* Romans 6:9-10 also addresses this by informing us that Christ will never die again because he is free from death's dominion, and the death he died was to sin, once and for all. So, Christ cannot be sacrificed anew. Likewise, Hebrews 9:26-27 makes it clear that Christ does not offer himself or suffer repeatedly for sin. Furthermore, the debt for sin has been paid (Col. 2:14), divine justice has been satisfied (Rom. 8:1), God's wrath has been poured out on Christ (1 Thess. 1:10, 5:9), and the elect have been propitiated (Rom. 3:25; Heb. 2:17; 1 John 2:2, 4:10) and justified (Rom. 3:24, 5:9). Logically, if Christ continues to suffer for sin, as observed in the Mass, then the payment for sin has never been fully paid. Sinners have not been redeemed, propitiated, or justified.

The efficacy of Christ's crucifixion and suffering is unbound and unfading in time since new believers throughout time are ransomed by the shed blood (Rev. 5:9) of his physical body, propitiated by it (Rom. 3:25), justified by it (Rom. 5:9), and the saints continue to be sprinkled by it (Heb. 10:22, 12:24). Therefore, there is no purgatory in which believers must suffer to make up for what is lacking in Christ's atonement for sin.

After Christ died in the flesh, he was *made alive in the spirit* (v. 18; Rom. 8:11). The Greek word πνεύματι (pneumati) does not distinguish between spirit and Spirit. The KJV renders this *made alive by the Spirit*, as does NASB in a footnote, and as we will see shortly, the Holy Spirit is inferred by the context of ensuing verses. This expresses Christ's victory over sin, death, and the grave (1 Tim. 3:16). It speaks of the Father's satisfaction and acceptance of Christ's sacrifice for sin and its expiation. Peter brings us to the cross—the emblem of suffering, the tomb—the emblem of death, and then elevates our hearts to the risen Lord, our hope of rest.

Peter explains that Christ's suffering and death were "*that he might bring us to God.*" The Greek reads *so that you (singular) he might bring to God.* Since Peter is writing to elect Jews, we may conclude that the unrighteous for whom Christ died are the elect, those particularly chosen by God. There is a real sense of a particular nature to all that Peter is writing about. Indeed, Christ suffered and died for sin, and by doing so, he brought the elect to the Father (John 14:6). Christ did not die to create a way or means for people to freely choose or reject to follow on their own accord. Peter allows for no ambiguity or alternative outcome. We thus conclude that Christ's obedience, suffering, and death were to bring the elect to God, not to make it possible on the precondition of faith, but to fully accomplish it.

Christ brings us to God but must first make us clean and acceptable to God. The unrighteous elect are declared righteous by the external, forensic righteousness of Christ being imputed to them so that they are legally righteous, that is justified (Rom. 3:23-24; 1 Cor. 6:11). The faith that is manifested by the elect bears witness to their righteous standing before God (Rom. 3:26; Col.1:21-22). The elect are not brought to God individually or in their intermediate state. The perfected church is presented on the last day when the elect are resurrected in soul and body (Rev. 21:22-27).

Since Christ's suffering has expiated our sins, why does it remain necessary for us to suffer? Our suffering is not for further expiation, nor could it be. Rather, it is to drive us to Christ, to secure and maintain our hope in him alone, that we may find our eternal security and comfort in his kindness to us and not in this world. John reminds us that the world is passing away, but we will abide with God forever if we do his will (1 John 2:17), for which we need the mercy and grace of the Son.

1 Peter 3:19

The spirits in prison

So, it was in the Holy Spirit that Christ proclaimed to the spirits in prison. Here, the King James Bible is truer to the Greek, as it uses the word "*preached*" instead of "*proclaimed.*" Peter is not listing events in sequential order. We should not assume that Christ rose from the dead first and then preached the Gospel to spirits in prison. Peter refers to a time before Christ's resurrection and his incarnation. He is merely stating that it was the same Spirit by which Jesus rose and through whom he preached to the spirits in prison. The next verse gives credence to this, and we may sort out what Peter means.

1 Peter 3:20

Because they formerly did not obey

We are pulled back in time to examine the days of Noah. Scripture informs us that Noah was a herald or preacher of righteousness (2 Pet. 2:5) and thus condemned the world

(Heb. 11:7). Noah had special revelations of things to come, that is, the judgment of the flood (Matt. 24:37-39; Luke 17:26-28), and preached to those around him. No one listened to him and left themselves unaware of the impending destruction.

We can now unravel 1 Peter 3:19-20 and conclude that God [Christ], via the Holy Spirit acting through Noah, preached to the disobedient world in which he lived and who are now the spirits in prison having been condemned by their disobedience. As to what Peter means by prison, I suggest it is the lower part of Hades (Matt. 11:23; Luke 10:15, 16:22-24; Acts 2:27) where the separated souls of the reprobate are held until the day of judgment. The flood was the means of their destruction and emblematic of the divine judgment against them.

It is estimated that Noah worked on building the ark for more than 100 years (Gen. 6:3). Peter makes note of God's patience during this time, not that he was patient with Noah but that he was patient with the world.

Multiple conclusions can be drawn from verse 20.

1. Noah labored for a long time to build the ark. Certainly, there was suffering involved in such labor, and it was likely from people in his surroundings, given the strangeness of the work he was engaged in, his righteousness, and his preaching. But his suffering was not for naught since its fruit, as ordained by God, was the deliverance of himself and his family through

the devastating flood.

2. Peter draws our attention to Noah's otherwise impossible deliverance, not from but through the flood (2 Pet. 2:5). Most importantly, Noah's deliverance through the deluge preserved the lineage of the promised seed of the woman (Gen. 3:15). Although we may not experience a similar deliverance from our suffering in this life, we can be assured of an eternal blessing and rest if we obey God. (Note: obedience does not lead to eternal life. Obedience is only possible by God's grace and is the basis of our assurance.)

3. We should not presume that God will, in all circumstances, be patient with disobedience nor ever test his patience. As Peter writes about God's patience in Noah's days, we should understand him to mean that God was mercifully patient with the sinful world by delaying the judgment of the flood until Noah completed the ark. Noah could proclaim warning and deliverance to the watching world because of God's patience and Christ's Spirit in him. Their refusal to listen to Noah was a refusal to heed the Spirit of Christ speaking through Noah (1 Pet. 3:19). We may conclude:

   (a) The world, apart from Noah and his family, was under the dominion of sin (John 8:34; Rom. 6:14-18).

(b) God's patience demonstrates his longsuffering (Exo. 34:6; Num. 14:18; Rom. 2:4; 2 Pet. 3:9).

(c) The judgment that was to come upon them was altogether righteousness.

Verses 19 and 20 are complex and compact. As we have attempted to unpack their content and explore their consequences, let's review and attempt to highlight what Peter's focus was for us as he wrote these verses. He has given us two examples of obedience during suffering and extraordinary deliverance. In both examples, sin is judged and condemned. Indeed, finding God's grace in these examples of deliverance is not difficult. It is especially the case in these examples that we recognize that suffering is necessary even if we do not see its immediate purpose or are freed from it in this life. There is a great consolation for the soul, knowing that Christ suffered on our behalf more than we ever will and has compassion for us as we suffer. Embedded in verses 19 and 20, we also discover the preaching of grace in the Old Testament and the presence of the Spirit of Christ active in judgment and deliverance.

1 Peter 3:21

Baptism

Peter perceives that what Noah experienced during the flood could be figuratively called baptism. By the deliverance of God, Noah passed through God's judgment against sin. But Peter is not referring to baptism figuratively. He is referring to the real spiritual baptism of the elect. The death of the old nature as it is mortified through Christ's death on the cross, becoming dead to the power of sin, and rising to new life with a new nature with the risen Lord, and living to God. This is the only baptism that saves you and does so through the resurrection of Jesus Christ (Rom. 6:4; Col. 2:11-12). From verse 18, Peter assures us that our suffering is linked to our deliverance from sin, and as we can be certain of the necessity and certainty of the latter, we can be certain of the necessity of the former. God fully delivers his people from sin's power and consequences while condemning sin in his own Son.

As an appeal to God for a good conscience

Peter has written that Noah's passing through the flood figuratively corresponds to our dying to sin and our spiritual baptism to new life. So that we do not confuse the reality of this baptism with the sacrament, he explains that the sacrament, in which one is immersed in water, removes nothing more than dirt when it is not joined with that which the sacrament signifies. Whereas the reality of that which the sacrament signifies saves and is an appeal of a good conscience before God. This appeal of a good conscience before God may be linked with our justification (Rom. 4:22-25), for without being justified, we cannot have a good conscience before God (Titus 1:15; Heb. 9:14).

The cross, that is, the death of Christ, does not complete our salvation. Christ's resurrection is necessary. Peter sees its necessity for how we may stand before God with a good conscience. As Paul writes, it is the basis for our justification (Rom. 4:25). The apostles agree that baptism is dying and rising with Christ, both necessary for salvation. Peter has a further purpose for us in mind: to free our conscience of the unnecessary guilt we may carry of former sins that we have repented of and may now hinder our joy in the Lord and the assurance of our salvation (Ps. 103:11-12; Rom. 8:1; Col. 2:13-14).

The recollection of former sins drives us to these declarations of God of our forgiveness through Jesus Christ so that by faith and with reverent fear, we may be assured of God's *"steadfast love toward those who fear him"* (Ps. 103:11), that he has canceled *"the record of debt that stood against us"* (Col. 2:14), and that *"there is therefore now no condemnation for those who are in Christ Jesus"* (Rom. 8:1). Since God has set the guilt of all our sins upon Jesus Christ (1 Pet. 2:24; Heb. 9:26) and raised him from the dead so that the debt we formerly owed has been paid in full by Jesus, we may know that we have an appeal of a good conscience before God, just as Peter wrote, and put to rest any apprehension of lingering guilt. As it is written, *"...let us also lay aside every weight, and sin which clings so closely, and let us run with endurance the race that is set before us."* (Heb. 12:1 ESV); and also, *"Let us then with confidence draw near to the throne of grace, that we may receive mercy and find grace to help in time of need."* (Heb. 4:16 ESV).

1 Peter 3:22

Who has gone into heaven

This is pure praise of Jesus Christ, and rightly so, following what Peter has written. It draws our minds to the glory, power, majesty, and supremacy of Jesus Christ. We must always be reminded of who he is, where he is, his power, majesty, and authority. It is in our nature to be forgetful, and by not renewing our minds about the things we have been taught concerning the faith, we tend to drift from them (Heb. 2:1; Rom. 12:2).

Peter raises our thoughts to the one we must deal with, demonstrating the necessity of submission and obedience and placing our trust, hope, and security in him alone.

In verse 22, Peter is dealing with the present. He presents a picture of Jesus Christ on the Father's right side in heaven. First, let us assess what he wrote about Jesus Christ, the incarnate divine person who is fully man and God, presently in his glorified state. By writing Jesus Christ and not Christ, Peter ensures we notice the man on the Father's side. If we notice this, we become keenly aware of the divine Person's compassion, sympathy, and kindness because he has suffered the manifold temptations that human nature is exposed to and has overcome them without sin. It also speaks of the preeminence of Christ and being the firstborn of all creation (Col. 1:15-20).

Jesus is at the right hand of God. "*At the right hand*" is a figure of speech that implies preeminence, authority, and being a representative. Although Peter, in his usual brevity, does not write it out for us, he prompts us to investigate the implications of what it means to be "the right-hand man of God." Elsewhere in Scripture, there are insights into what Jesus Christ does from heaven.

1. Jesus is in the presence of God on our behalf (Heb. 9:24).

2. He is a minister in his holy temple (Heb. 8:1-2).

3. He intercedes and saves to the uttermost for those who draw near to God through him (Heb. 7:23-25; Rom. 8:34).

4. He sustains all creation (Heb. 1:3).

5. He is our only mediator between us and God (1 Tim. 2:5).

6. He is the head of the church (Eph. 5:23).

Verse 22 and Chapter 3 close with *"angels, authorities, and powers having been subjected to him."* Peter intends that we remain secure in our faith and that through Jesus Christ, our hope of salvation is secure. We are drawn to contemplate that angels are subject to the man Jesus Christ. Paul expresses Peter's concept in more detail and clarity in Ephesians 1:19-23. The Father worked his power on our behalf through Jesus Christ. The Father raised him from the dead (for our justification) and seated him at his right hand in heaven. All rule, authority, power, dominion, and every name now and forever has been put under and subjected to Christ, who is head over all things to the church. There is no power by which we may be removed from the love of Christ, for all power is subject to him (Rom. 8:38-39, 11:29)

While verse 22 is a statement of praise, it is to our benefit that we may more surely know the necessity of our obedience and the security of our hope and trust in the Lord Jesus Christ. Surely, Jesus will be our deliverance from the sufferings we endure, and we will find our eternal rest and comfort in him alone.

Chapter 3 Summary

The principle focus of Chapter 3 is Christian relationships and how they are to be managed and maintained by our conduct. These relationships are presented in a sequence that begins with the private relation of marriage, then expands to church members, and culminates with general interactions with all people. While relationships and conduct are the focus, Peter draws our thoughts to Christ as the impetus for good conduct that comes from a sanctified heart. The apostle instructs women about submission to their husbands, which brings them great blessings. They become precious in God's sight with an imperishable beauty and are regarded as holy women. Husbands are to honor their wives, for they are coheirs of the same grace of life. Attached is a warning that failure in this will lead to godly discipline.

Peter exhorts all individuals within the church to have unity of mind, sympathy, brotherly love, and a humble mind. We are instructed that we shouldn't precipitate or promote evil against another person but always seek and pursue peace. He urges us to continue to sanctify our hearts and to focus on the hope given to us by grace so that we may be prepared to answer anyone who asks why we have such hope. Our first and perhaps primary witness of this hope is how we conduct ourselves in relationships with spouses, fellow believers, and the world. A memorable passage in Chapter 3:

But in your hearts honor Christ the Lord as holy, always being prepared to make a defense to anyone who asks you for a reason

for the hope that is in you; yet do it with gentleness and respect,
(1 Pet. 3:15 ESV)

Peter closes the chapter by returning to doctrine, reminding us of the Father's power to us through Jesus Christ and the supremacy of Christ. There are many treasures of the knowledge of God and Jesus Christ in these few verses. They speak to us of our utter dependency on the love of our heavenly Father and the Lord Jesus Christ and the security of our hope for eternal rest.

Chapter 4 – Guarded Through Faith

Introduction

In this chapter on Christian Suffering, Peter outlines various reasons we may suffer. Whether we suffer at the hands of acquaintances or fiery trials, all suffering is according to the will of God. This text poses an implied question: do you suffer in a Christ-honoring manner? Peter leads us into episodes of self-examination so that we may endure whatever suffering comes upon us with a good conscience before God and an unshakable assurance of the hope to which we have been called.

4:1-3 Thinking Like Christ

How are we, as elect children of God, supposed to deal with sin in our own lives? Peter answers this question in two ways by bringing us to Christ's suffering for sin and how Jesus regarded sin. First, Christ suffered for our sins only while he was in the flesh. The time Jesus was in the flesh has passed, so he no longer suffers for our sins. The time for our suffering for sin has also passed because we no longer live according to our former nature. Second, as we now live for the will of God, we can confront the temptations to sin with the *mind of Christ*." As we think like Christ did about temptation and sin, we will be more apt to refrain.

The apostles have used different arguments to convey the same exhortations. Here, Peter uses a pastoral approach to instruct the saints to refrain from sin. Paul, meanwhile, writes as a father, laying it on the line to Timothy. We need to hear this from both Peter and Paul.

> But God's firm foundation stands, bearing this seal: "The Lord knows those who are his," and, "Let everyone who names the name of the Lord depart from iniquity" (2 Tim. 2:19 ESV).

1 Peter 4:1

Christ suffered in the flesh

Peter's phrase, "Christ suffered in the flesh," has a special meaning. As we have seen in 1 Peter 3:18, Christ suffered for sin once (Rom. 6:10; Heb. 7:27, 9:26, 28); we now add that this was fully accomplished while in the flesh. The entire content and extent of Christ's suffering was for sin and completed while he was in the flesh. While the person Jesus Christ is the same divine person in heaven as he was physically on earth, he is no longer in the flesh since his natural body has become a spiritual body (1 Cor. 15:44). He no longer suffers for sin to expiate or propitiate it as the redeemer of the elect (1 Pet. 3:18). 1 Peter 3:18 and 4:1 have a bearing on the practice and meaning of the Lord's Supper. The grace conferred during the Lord's Supper is not for the expiation of sin. Christ does not suffer in, by, or through the Sacrament to expiate sin that he has already effectually expiated. The Lord's Supper is a means of grace by which believers are spiritually strengthened and nourished as they contemplate the efficacy of Christ's death, its manifold benefits to believers, their union with him (1 Cor. 10:16), their communion with the saints (1 Cor. 10:17, 12:13), and the sure promise of his coming again in glory (1 Cor.

11:26). Since the Roman Catholic Mass is an observance of Christ's ongoing suffering for sin, it cannot withstand the scrutiny of Scripture.

Peter argues that since Christ's suffering for sin is over and done, so should ours. But for us, the suffering due to sin is avoided or defeated by no longer living in it. We have come to a new life with new abilities.

Having already established in Chapter 3 that Christ suffered once for sin, Peter directs our minds to it with the appeal that we should be armed with the same mind as Christ. In what way, then, should we be thinking? Christ died and rose to bring us to God. He couldn't just bring us to God without first making us legally holy and righteous; thus, his death and resurrection freed us from the guilt and power of sin. There was a purpose for Christ's suffering, and we should realize there is a purpose for ours. As Christ was sinless in all things, Peter exhorts us that, with the mind of Christ, we should strive to refrain from sin as we leave the manner of our former lives and now live for God.

For clarification, Jesus Christ is the same divine person now as he was during his earthly ministry. At that former time, Jesus was in the flesh with a physical body (Rom. 8:3; Eph 2:14; Col. 1:22; 1 Tim. 3:16; Heb. 2:14; 5:7, 10:5, 10; 1 Pet. 2:24; 3:18; 1 John 4:2; 2 John 1:7). However, when Jesus ascended, his physical body of flesh became a spiritual body raised in glory and power and imperishable (1 Cor. 15:42-44). The belief that Jesus Christ continues to suffer to expiate sin repudiates the efficacy of Christ's atonement, denies the word of God, demeans the glorious state to which Jesus Christ has ascended, and leaves the believer with no assurance of being saved.

Arm yourselves with the same way of thinking

Let us first consider why Christ suffered in the flesh. He was put to death for our sins (1 Cor. 15:3). Recalling verse 3:18, it was to bring us, the elect, to God. Sin kept us apart from God, so Christ suffered in the flesh unto death to free us from sin and made us fit to be brought to God. Peter calls us to align our thinking with Christ's about suffering, particularly his suffering and how he dealt with it, so that we will be of like mind and conduct when we suffer.

Peter immediately connects the purpose of Christ's suffering with sin, our sin, and claims that if we think and act like Christ, especially when it is most challenging in times of suffering, we will stop sinning. We must explore what he means by thinking like Christ and ceasing from sin. By calling believers to think like Christ, Peter encourages us to engage our minds in a manner or mode they are quite capable of. Believers have been born again and possess a new nature, which Paul calls *the mind of Christ* (1 Cor. 2:16). The natural man is in a tangle of human passions. He does not accept and cannot understand the things of the Spirit of God because they are spiritually discerned (1 Cor. 2:14) and lacks the "*mind of Christ.*" The natural man cannot think like Christ about suffering and sin.

The Greek word πέπαυται (pepautai) is usually translated in Scripture as *ceased* or a similar meaning. But believers still sin (1 John 1:8-10). We must understand that Peter's statement about sin is not a general principle but is limited by the context of the verse. Believers who do not conduct themselves as Christ when they suffer are sinning. Those who guide their conduct through suffering by thinking like Christ refrain from sinning. That is only part of Peter's point; we must go to the next verse to complete it.

1 Peter 4:2

Live for the rest of the time in the flesh

Here, we must be careful. The phrase *"living in the flesh"* is elsewhere symbolic of sinful living (Rom. 7:5), which is not what Peter means by *"live for the rest of time in the flesh."* He uses these words for the remaining time of our lives while we are still in this world, as did Paul (Gal. 2:20). When referring to the flesh, note that the passions of the flesh still tempt us, but having the mind of Christ toward sin, we no longer live for these passions (Rom. 8:4-6). Instead, we live for the will of God. The will of God is contrasted with men's desires as is more clearly seen in the Greek text. The conclusions of both Paul and Peter are the same; while in the flesh, we live by faith in the Son of God, which is the will of God.

If we truly have the mind of Christ, that is, to think like Christ against sin, we possess two things. First, we have the desire and ability to live for God rather than for the pleasures of sin. Second, we are no longer slaves to sin, and sin has lost its power over us (Rom. 6:17). Even though we continue to sin, we are not living in it and know that our redeemer intercedes for us as we confess our sins with sincere repentance. When we strive to think like Christ, grace is imparted by which we cease sinning (Rom. 6:14).

The doctrine of election is typically misrepresented by the claim that people who believe in election think they can live any way that pleases them and yet go to heaven when they die. Election is a Biblical doctrine that Peter and Paul wrote about (Rom. 9:11, 11:28; 2 Pet. 1:10). The clear and unambiguous teaching of Scripture is that the elect are a particular people (Matt. 1:21; Luke 1:68, 77; 1 Cor. 1:24), chosen by the Father (Col. 3:12; Eph. 1:4; 1 Pet. 2:9), called to Christ (Rom. 1:6, 7; Gal. 1:6; Col. 3:15; 2 Thess. 2:14; 1 Pet. 5:10), and without exception, raised to glory when Christ appears (John 6:39, 44; Rom. 8:21; 1 Cor. 15:42-44; 2 Cor. 4:14; Eph. 2:6). The Bible teaches that people can confirm their calling and election if they live a life of faith and walk according to the Spirit (2 Pet. 1:5-10; Rom. 8:4-6). Otherwise, they have no assurance that they are among God's chosen people.

1 Peter 4:3

For the time that is past

Peter has more to tell us about ceasing from sin, using verse 3 to underscore verses 1 and 2. The time for sinning is over. All sin committed during our former life was sufficiently contained in the past and remains there, as does our former nature. This is parallel to Christ's suffering for sin while in the flesh. He is no longer in the flesh, as we no longer live according to our former nature. The present and future have no space in them for living in the sins of the past.

Peter briefly lists several representative examples of typical sins his readers, and us by extension, would be familiar with and which many likely have engaged in. He declares that these sins are what the Gentiles [still] want to do. The Gentiles' desire arises from their nature because they *live in* them as an attribute of their nature. But for his elect readers, Peter is telling us that we no longer live in them because that time has passed for us.

Is Peter telling us that all Gentiles live in sensuality, passion, drunkenness, orgies, drinking parties, and lawless idolatry? He is using the title or term Gentiles to refer only to those who live in a way that is usually attributed to Gentiles, especially by the Jews he is writing to. It is a figure of speech, a metonymy. Here, Gentiles refers to the appetite for debauchery, which they are generally known for. But even more so, Peter, in verses 2:12 and 4:3, is making those he is writing to, Jews who returned from captivity and are dispersed throughout Asia Minor and now living among Gentiles, consider their sins as they have been living like Gentiles all the while. His purpose is to demonstrate their shame and, all the more, drive them to Christ.

Paul's extensive writings about Gentiles are quite pastoral and inclusive (Gal. 3:8). But he also refers to Gentiles with the same figure of speech (Eph. 4:17). Is Paul writing that all Gentiles walk in the futility of their minds, or that all

Gentiles will be justified by faith? No. In Ephesians 4:17, he intends for us to think of the reputation Gentiles have become known by. In Galatians 3:8, he intends us to think of specific prophesies of Scripture and the promise to Abraham and explicitly states so in the verse.

4:4-7 Judgment Is Ready "Why the Gospel Is Preached"

In these verses, Peter first has us reflect on how we lived before having faith in Christ. He has us admit that we lived as sinfully as the pagan world does. However, that time and that way of life are in our past, and we are not to live in it any longer. We are exhorted to think like Christ, not only about suffering but about living according to the will of God. He acknowledges that believers will suffer at the hands of former friends who want us to return to that life of debauchery and warns us not to. We are told that those who malign us will be called to account as Peter brings our focus to the day of judgment and warns us to be sober-minded. He clarifies that death does not separate the departed soul from the Lordship of Christ.

1 Peter 4:4

With respect to this

Peter is pursuing a timeline. It begins in the past when you (his collective Jewish readers) lived among the Gentiles and lived in the passions of the flesh like Gentiles. We cannot disassociate ourselves from Peter's immediate audience as we were in many ways like them before being drawn to Christ.

What he refers to as the Gentile manner of life in his day, we may think of as the pagan, secular society surrounding the church today. Now you no longer live like the Gentiles, though in the past you did, as he says in the flesh. In 1 Peter 2:12, he exhorted, *"Keep your conduct among the Gentiles honorable..."* While still living among the Gentiles, you can no longer live like them. Henceforth, you are to think like Christ and sin no more. Likewise, today, we are living with a new nature and new spiritual abilities by which we live in *"the will of God"* (1 Pet. 4:2). Of course, being a Jew and being reminded of your former sins and the Gentiles' reputation at the same moment would cause considerable shame.

They are surprised

Peter is writing to his collective readers using the plural *you* but the impact of his writing falls upon his readers individually. Let us put ourselves in the minds of his Jewish audience as we study this verse. The Gentiles you have been living among are still Gentiles who live in the passions of the flesh. Gentiles, expecting you to join them, as you have in the past, in whatever debauchery they plan and discover your absence. They don't understand why you no longer participate, so they investigate. What they discover is a surprise, something they don't expect because it is foreign to their minds, your new manner of life or way of living.

They malign you

A person is maligned when someone speaks in a purposefully harmful and defaming way about them, using slander and outright lies. Peter is not warning his readers to be on the lookout for this to avoid it. Rather, he acknowledges that they are currently suffering this way from their former associates. The converted Jews didn't need to seek out their former Gentile associates to reprove them. Just how they now conducted themselves was a sufficient reproof to invoke this evil against them (Pro. 9:7-8). We should wisely consider that whenever we resist participating in the evil of the current godless world or cast light on their debauchery, we will be maligned for our faith and good conduct with potentially harmful results.

1 Peter 4:5

Give an account

There should be no doubt that the *"him"* referred to is Jesus Christ. Peter has instructed his readers that suffering is expected and necessary but that God will guide them through these difficulties through faith. In verses 4:1-3, he encouraged them to practice godly lives by exhorting them that the time during which they formerly lived in the passions of the flesh has ceased. Then, in verse 4:4, Peter acknowledged their continued suffering at the hands of evil men, even their former associates. The righteous may ask, "Is there no end to our suffering?" "Will the wicked prevail in their debauchery and cruelty?" "Will there be no relief, no justification of the righteous?" These questions are not unusual or indicative of a stumbling faith. To strengthen our faith, God acknowledges our questions and reminds us he is always in control.

The judgment of the wicked in Habakkuk's days, as has happened at other times in history, was only a foretaste of the judgment Peter refers to. He realizes that people suffering at the hands of others need to know that justice will have its day, and he is referring directly to the day of judgment when Christ appears with his mighty angels, and all wickedness and evil will come to an end. Peter's meaning is twofold. First, those suffering need to know that the wicked at whose hands they suffer will be judged for all their wickedness. Second, they need to know that should they seek to end their suffering by returning to their former ways, they will invoke the same judgment upon themselves.

The wicked maligners will give their account to the Lord on the day of judgment. Peter positively assures us that the wicked will be judged, from which we may imply that the account they render will not be sufficient to vindicate themselves. But we should not think based on this that they alone will give an account (Heb. 4:13).

Ready to judge

Jesus Christ is ready even now to judge all mankind. He is not more ready today to judge mankind than in Peter's day. We are never to think judgment is delayed, for we are told that Jesus Christ is ready at this very moment to come and judge all mankind. Peter intends to invoke in our minds the need to be ready to meet the Lord in judgment, even now. Do not think you can return to your former friends for a season and engage in the same debauchery, for the Lord holds all people to give an account when he returns unannounced

(Luke 12:40).

The living and the dead

The phrase "*living and the dead*" does not refer to the spiritually alive and spiritually dead. These terms refer to the physically alive and the physically dead, all mankind alive or dead. This establishes that Christ's power and authority extend beyond the grave and that those who have passed away remain subjects of his Lordship and accountable to him. This is a great solace to the saints, knowing they will still be the Lord's should they pass away and that physical death does not separate them from the Lord. The one who judges is the divine person, Jesus Christ, fully God and fully man, appointed by the Father to judge all mankind (John 5:22, 27; Acts 10:42; 2 Tim. 4:1). The grave is no escape from judgment or separation from the Lord.

1 Peter 4:6

Why the gospel was preached

Peter is giving great consolation to the living saints in two ways. The first deals with believers who have passed away so that the living know these beloved saints are not lost or forsaken. Secondly, the living believers can be assured of the same security in the Lord if they die before the Lord returns.

Why was the gospel preached to the dead? It was not preached to people after they died; it was preached to them when they were alive but who are now dead. Though men may judge the dead as nothing but corpses, they are alive unto

God by the power of the gospel. The gospel is the revelation of Jesus Christ, who fulfilled the covenantal promise that God would send a savior and provide a sacrifice for sin. The power of this gospel to save is not overthrown by death, as some have claimed. Peter is pointing out, against such claims, that the gospel was preached to saints who have since passed away so that now, being physically dead and their bodies in graves, they are alive by the power of the gospel, living in the spirit. He refers to the spirits or souls of the saints who have gone to be with God. The soul that is preserved by faith through death lives in the spirit the same way God does (Heb. 10:39). Likewise, Paul informs us that the souls of the saints who have passed away are with the Lord and will be with him when he appears in judgment on the last day (1 Thess. 4:13-14). What amazing comfort this is to contemplate when suffering the judgments of men for our faith and being concerned for our loved ones who have passed away.

While we are in the flesh, there is a manner in which we currently live or are to live as saints. The saints live by and according to the Spirit, keeping our minds on the things of the Spirit (Gal. 5:25; Rom. 8:5). Peter will refer to the spirits of men as souls in verse 4:19.

1 Peter 4:7

The end of all things is at hand

Two phrases are used in Scripture: *"the end of the ages"* and *"the end of the age."* The first refers to the last age in a series of ages. This is the age, the last age, or the age during which we live (1 Cor. 10:11). The second phrase refers to the end of the last age (Matt. 13:40).

Peter is drawing our attention to the end of the present age, which, as he explains, is *"the end of all things"* and that this end is *"at hand."* The phrase *"at hand"* means that it is imminent. He is referencing the last day, when all things end, to engender a sense of urgency and necessity to order our lives in a righteous and godly manner. As we work out Peter's words, we see that he is referring to the end of all things that can be made, shaken, and are perishable as opposed to that which cannot be shaken and are imperishable (Heb. 12:25-29). However, he is causing us to contemplate how imminent this is. Like him, the author of Hebrews concludes that this should make us grateful and offer God acceptable worship, reverence, and awe.

Peter returns to this urgent message in his second epistle with more detail. The end of all things will occur on a day when it is not expected. Destruction will be by fire, and all things will be dissolved (2 Pet. 3:10-12). As we wait for the time when all perishable things come to an end, on the last day of the last days, we are instructed with genuine urgency to live *lives of holiness and godliness* (2 Pet.3:11), *be on guard, keep awake* (Mark 13:33). Here, Peter adds instructions to be *self-controlled and sober-minded.*

Be self-controlled

How can one control the passions of the flesh, the temptations that have enslaved mankind in sin, so that he can live in holiness and godliness? Peter claims this is done by self-control. Even now, while we live in the flesh, we have abilities of the soul lacking in the natural man. To improve these abilities, we must exercise them. The saints can resist sinning, not perfectly, but they can resist far better than any natural man and certainly more so than during their former lives. Being sober-minded goes along with self-control, for the right-thinking person understands the consequences of his choices and can deduce which is right, proper, and aligned with the will of God. The sober-minded saint also understands the urgency of Peter's message and the nature of his times.

Peter calls us to be sober-minded three times in this epistle, in verses 1:13; 4:7; and 5:8. Paul also exhorts overseers, their wives, and older men to be sober-minded (1 Tim. 3:2, 11; 2 Tim. 4:5; Tit. 2:2). All the saints are called to sober-mindedness, but Paul highlights its importance as he primarily directs elders and ministers to this. In contrast to a sober mind is the futile mind (Eph. 4:17), which leads people into ungodliness as they walk according to the flesh.

For the sake of your prayers

Peter, anticipating the potential of a laissez-faire reaction to the urgency of the times in which we live, adds the caveat that being self-controlled and sober-minded has a bearing on our prayers. We should understand that he implies that our prayers will be hindered, as stated in 1 Peter 3:7 of husbands who do not honor their wives. This is a spiritual condition. Living a self-controlled life with a sober mind is a necessity to which the saints have been called. It cannot be faked and must arise from within, so our prayers will be deficient if these qualities are lacking.

Peter states the obvious: who can pray rightly without being sober-minded and self-controlled? In Paul's discourse on the whole armor of God, he tells us to *take the helmet of salvation... praying at all times* (Eph. 6:17-18). Considering where you wear a helmet and what it protects, Paul is alluding to being right-minded in God's word, which enables us to pray in the Spirit.

4:8-11 In Everything, God May Be Glorified

Peter will return to the theme of suffering but will spend the following several verses on Christian living and conduct among the saints. It is parallel in many ways to Chapter 13 of Romans. These are important verses. It is not sufficient to spiritually care for yourself and only your relationship with the Lord. Peter provides the proper perspective that we live for each other, not unto ourselves only.

1 Peter 4:8

Above all, keep loving one another earnestly

Of paramount importance is love for each other with sincere love from the heart. Peter is turning his attention to the welfare of the community of saints. Paul goes so far as to say anything done without being joined with love is of no personal gain (1 Cor. 13:1-3).

Peter does not claim that love is more important than being sober-minded or that self-control may be set aside to pursue love. Previously, he grouped brotherly love with unity of the mind, sympathy, a tender heart, and a humble mind (1 Pet. 3:8). He is presenting the importance of love as a remedy for a condition he has not yet but will shortly reveal.

Paul dealt with this condition in the church at Corinth, where he had to chastise them for quarreling, jealousy, anger, and other expressions of misconduct (2 Cor. 12:20). He described their behavior as inconsistent with the expected behavior within the household of God (1 Tim. 3:15).

Love covers a multitude of sins

Peter's remedy for the conduct occurring in the Corinthian church (a true multitude of sins), and presumably elsewhere, is love. He recognized that sinful behavior between brothers and sisters of the church springs from an absence of love. If we love our brothers and sisters, we will not engage in such behaviors as Paul had to admonish at Corinth. If we return love to our brothers and sisters who sin against us, their sinning may stop. When sin is prevented or stopped by love, it is covered (Pro. 10:12) and is no longer the source of strife.

1 Peter 4:9

Show hospitality to one another

Among the saints, each is to be hospitable to one another without muttering or murmuring. The word *show* is not in the

Greek text. Its presence in the English translation might wrongly be taken to mean that our hospitality to one another should be a matter of display. Indeed not. Peter is exhorting us to display genuine hospitality that is not hypocritical. When hospitality is accompanied by complaints, muttering, or murmuring, it does a disservice to the church and harms its recipient's reputation. This appeal is well placed in the text as it follows our calling to love one another earnestly from the heart, which we may find most challenging in some instances. At this moment, Peter offers no excuse to us to withhold anything our brothers and sisters may need if we have the means to provide it, including our love with all sincerity. Genuine hospitality follows from a heartfelt love for the saints, individually and collectively.

1 Peter 4:10

Each has received a gift

Peter establishes that each member of the church has received a gift. What sort of gift is he referring to? As usual, he leaves us to turn to the other epistles for details. Although Paul lists more specific gifts than Peter, neither is comprehensive (Rom. 12:4-8; 1 Cor. 12:4-11). These lists of gifts include:

Prophecy	knowledge	*These gifts have ceased with the passage of the Apostolic Age.
service	Faith	
teaching	healing*	

exhortation	working	
generosity	miracles*	
leadership	discernment	
mercy	tongues*	
wisdom	interpretation	

Both Peter and Paul agree that the gifts are for the common good and that we should not withhold their use. We should understand and conclude that we are merely *stewards* of these gifts by God's grace, not for us alone but for the whole church. The grace verse 10 refers to is God's continued unmerited goodness to us that follows receiving his special grace of regeneration. Peter describes it as "*varied*," for it produces different gifts and abilities among the saints, which are effectuated through various manifestations of the Holy Spirit.

Giving and administering gifts is an important work of the Holy Spirit. The Spirit's work includes equipping men with the necessary gifts for evangelism, shepherding, and teaching. This strengthens and unifies the church and protects it from human cunning and deceitful schemes (Eph. 4:11-16). The work of the Holy Spirit is extensive, giving us access to the Father as members of his household. We are collectively becoming a holy temple in the Lord, and it occurs through Jesus Christ. The giving and administration of gifts by the Holy Spirit are for these purposes.

1 Peter 4:11

Whoever speaks or serves

Peter directs our minds to the source, power, and purpose of our gifts so that we do not become puffed up with prideful notions about ourselves. If one speaks, teaches, or preaches from the Bible, he is reminded by Peter that the words of scripture are God's words, as are their meaning, purpose, and fruit (2 Pet. 1:20-21).

If one serves or ministers, Peter reminds him that it is not according to his own strength but by the strength granted by God. Although he only brings these two gifts to the forefront, what is true of them is true of all of the gifts God gives so that, in all cases, our minds and hearts are drawn to God, glorifying him through Jesus Christ in everything.

To him belong glory and honor

The closing phrase of verse 4:11 is a doxology. It is in the most wonderful place. God's gracious gifts and the fruit they produce are so precious and wonderful that they incite the apostle to immediate praise as they are brought to mind. There is a special necessity for such doxologies in Scripture. Because of the dullness of our minds, we constantly need to be reminded that glory and honor belong to God, neither of which we should ever claim or seek for ourselves, though it is our propensity to do so.

As for these spiritual gifts, we must never use them for our aggrandizement. Peter emphasizes this in two ways. First,

God's glory and dominion are to the ages of the ages, as it is written in Greek. Forever is "to the age of the age," a singular age multiplied by a singular age. Forever and ever is "to the ages of the ages," a plural of ages multiplied by a plural of ages. It is more than a simple emphasis. Instead, it is a distinction of something with no beginning and no end. God's ownership of glory and dominion are as timeless as himself, and no matter how we try, we will not rob him of what he owns and will not share. Second, Peter adds, "Amen." which is "*so be it.*" It is as if he is warning us to take verse 11 with all seriousness, for it is immutably true.

Notice that verse 4:11 clearly states that God is glorified in all things. In the ESV bible, there is a period between the words *Jesus Christ* and *To him,* which does not appear in the KJV or NASB bibles. This raises the question of to whom "*him*" refers after the period. Does it refer to Jesus Christ or God? Let's examine how this verse is rendered in other translations.

If any man speak, let him speak as the oracles of God; if any man minister, let him do it as of the ability which God giveth: that God in all things may be glorified through Jesus Christ, to whom be praise and dominion for ever and ever. Amen (1 Pet. 4:11 KJV).

Whoever speaks is to do so as one who is speaking actual words of God; whoever serves is to do so as one who is serving by the strength which God supplies; so that in all things God may be glorified through Jesus Christ, to whom belongs the glory and dominion forever and ever. Amen (1 Pet. 4:11 NASB).

The glory and dominion are attributed to Jesus Christ since he is the immediate antecedent of "*whom*." The interlinear Greek text in this section of 4:11 is:

so that in all things may be glorified - God through Jesus Christ to whom be the glory and the power to the ages of the ages Amen (Greek Interlinear , biblehub.com).

Whether or not you interpret Peter's writing about glory and power as assigned to God or Jesus Christ, Peter does not intend for us to understand that it must be exclusively one or the other. The case has been made extensively throughout Scripture that glory, power, dominion, and majesty belong to Jesus Christ (Heb. 1:3; 2 Pet. 1:16; Jude 1:25).

4:12-16 Suffering Part 1 "Sharing Christ's Suffering"

The context of 1 Peter 4:12 -19 is suffering for the name of Christ, as earlier stated in verses 4:8-11 that Peter would return to this theme. His purpose in this entire section is for Christians to respond to suffering properly as Christians. He warns of an upcoming fiery trial, delineates between Christian and non-Christian responses, and then leads us to reflect on God's judgment to warn and vindicate the righteous.

1 Peter 4:12

The fiery trial

Peter begins verse 12 with the greeting, "Beloved." He uses this greeting for a purpose. The Jews of the dispersion to whom he is writing, and by extension us as well, are so regarded by God as to be to him his beloved. I do not take this to be an expression of Peter's affection, as no human affection could serve the purpose for which he is writing. This is at variance with Matthew Henry's comments on this greeting, whereas John Calvin does not comment on this greeting. What Peter is about to tell us is very troubling, so his writing is that of a caring pastor and comforter by informing us of the affection in God's heart for us. He is returning us to the subject of suffering, a topic he has not departed from, and as he does, he sets our minds on the contemplation of God's love for us. He then told us that a trial with the following characteristics will come upon us: it will be so severe as to be called fiery, and it will test us. By being called fiery, he does not mean it will be by fire but that it will be severe. We may also understand that what is being tested is our faith and that this test is the trial. Peter also instructs that we should not think of this as something strange, as if it should not be happening or somehow unnatural, but we should not be surprised by its occurrence. Thus, we should expect such a trial and be prepared for it. At this time, we may recall Paul's exposition of the full armor of God in Ephesians 6:10-18.

1 Peter 4:13

Rejoice

Peter outlines what our response should be when this trial comes upon us. We should rejoice. He has previously called us to rejoice in 1 Peter 1:6 and 1:8. In verse 1:8, he describes this rejoicing as inexpressible and filled with glory. It is something that cannot be explained to others or shared.

Elsewhere in Scripture, the saints are called to rejoice all the time (Phil 4:4; 1 Thess. 5:16).

As our rejoicing is in the Lord, it is a special type that the world cannot experience or participate in. However, Peter places a caveat on our rejoicing in this particular suffering. Though we suffer, our rejoicing should be genuinely due to our participation in Christ's suffering instead of rejoicing for worldly reasons. If our rejoicing is genuine, we have an even greater reason to rejoice when Christ reappears in glory. As to Christ's reappearing, it is not merely a glorious appearance or an appearance that is glorious. Rather, as Christ reappears, his essential glory will be manifest to all beings. John wrote about the glory that will appear when Christ comes with his saints (1 Thess. 3:13, 4:14) and mighty angels (Matt. 16:27, 25:31; Mark 8:38; 2 Thess. 1:7) and the glory that will appear with and in him.

The beloved saints, those Peter was writing to and those reading this, were then and are now God's children and will be like Jesus when we see him in his glory (1 John 3:2). This verse from John addresses the perseverance of the saints quite clearly. Only the saints from among all men will rejoice on the last day, and only the saints will be transformed by his glory.

Note that the saints already in heaven must appear with Christ so that their bodies may be raised first. Then, the saints left on earth will be raised, body and soul. Thus, all the saints will participate in the second resurrection and forever be with the Lord (1 Thess. 4:13-17). Paul writes of our rejoicing even now in the hope of this glory to be revealed (Rom. 5:2).

What greater comfort might there be for those who suffer in Christ but to know that God's love will guard them through all things unto the reappearing of Christ.

As you share Christ's suffering

To explain what Peter meant by writing, "*as you share Christ's suffering,*" recall what Jesus spoke to Paul on the road to Damascus (Acts 9:1-5). Paul was on a mission to persecute Christians, round them up, and bring them to Jerusalem as prisoners and very likely to be put to death. The Lord appeared to Paul and said, "*I am Jesus, whom you are persecuting.*"

When a saint is caused to suffer because he is a saint, because of his faith in Christ and his obedience to him, the bond of union between him and Christ Jesus is such that Jesus is also being persecuted, to use the language of Acts.

Paul, writing of his and Timothy's suffering, explains his extraordinary self-awareness as an apostle and their relation to the saints concerning suffering and comfort. He wrote of his suffering and comfort for Christ and the saints since there is a profound solidarity among them (2 Cor. 1:3-7). This is why Paul can say that he rejoices in his suffering to supply what is lacking in Christ's affliction (Col. 1:24). This Colossian verse does not mean there is any shortcoming to Christ's suffering and atonement. Because Christ suffers when his saints suffer, Paul rejoices because he can participate in it, as should we.

This is precisely what Peter meant by why we should rejoice for being participants in suffering with Christ. As we contemplate Christ's suffering in Isaiah, the Psalms, and the

Gospels, we may mistakenly think his suffering for sin didn't end by conflating it with the ongoing suffering that Christ endures in solidarity with us, for we should rejoice in being participants in it. However, we must realize Christ's continued suffering is not expiatory or propitiatory. Christ suffered once for sin (Heb. 9:24-28).

Peter's purpose is to provide comfort and assurance to saints because he knows they will suffer because they are saints. It is to them he is writing, or writing of. Nevertheless, there is a hidden warning in verse 12. Although all suffering is according to the will of God, not all suffering is in Christ. There is no cause to rejoice when suffering is not associated with Christ, and gives no cause to rejoice or be glad when Christ's glory is revealed. For details, we turn to Paul.

The righteous judgment of God has two parts. First, you are worthy of the kingdom if you suffer for it; second, those who afflict you will be repaid with affliction. You will receive relief, but those who did not obey the gospel will suffer eternal destruction (2 Thess. 1:5-10). Although Peter does not get into all that Paul does, our minds may be drawn to these things as we contemplate the implications of Peter's epistle. The saints have something secure and glorious to hope and look forward to with all expectation that the rest of mankind does not. Much more, what awaits the rest of the world is eternal destruction.

1 Peter 4:14

Insulted for the name of Christ

The pagan world needs nothing more than to see that we are associated with Christ to be abusive to us. We need not encourage them to do what is theirs by nature. The pagan world has hated Jesus and will hate you, his followers (John 15:18). This is one of the reasons why Peter in 1 Peter 2:13-14 exhorted believers to be submissive to all human institutions in so far as it is in the Lord to do so.

You are blessed

Being blessed is not due to having been afflicted for the name of Christ but because the Holy Spirit rests on you. The affliction you suffer in the name of Christ is a testimony to the blessing that the Holy Spirit rests on you. Peter draws our minds to the Spirit and God in a particular way. He denotes the Spirit as the Spirit of glory and that the glory is of God. The suffering he is writing about testifies to our participation in that blessed glory.

When Paul compares the ministry of the law to the ministry of the Spirit, he compares the glory of one to the glory of the other. The ministry of the law was a ministry of condemnation and of death but possessed such grace that the Israelites could not look upon Moses's face, which we may note merely reflected its glory. As that ministry has passed away, so has the glory thereof. But the ministry of the Spirit possesses even more glory as the ministry of righteousness does not perish (2 Cor. 3:7-11). The glory of the ministry of the Holy Spirit, which Paul writes about, is due to the essential glory of God and the Spirit that Peter writes of. Paul could not write of the glory of the ministry of the Spirit if he were not writing of the Spirit of glory. Verse 14 thus alludes to the indwelling of the Holy Spirit and his ministry of works to us from which we receive all manner of comfort, encouragement, strength, and endurance.

The King James Version is based on different Greek manuscripts and renders verse 14 as follows:

> *If ye be reproached for the name of Christ, happy are ye; for the spirit of glory and of God resteth upon you:* <u>*on their part he [Christ] is evil spoken of, but on your part he is glorified.*</u> (1 Pet. 4:14 KJV)

As you can see, the underlined section is not in the ESV Bible, NASB, or NIV. This additional phrase does not possess anything disagreeable with the context of the verse, the chapter, or the whole of Scripture. It is reasonably proposed that as manuscripts are copied, the text is more likely lost due to an accidental omission than being deliberately added or removed. The translation from Greek into English is also a concern because the results may reflect the theological biases of the translators. In both sets of manuscripts, the interlinear Greek text reads *if you are insulted in [the]name of Christ.* This seems consistent with the additional text in the KJV, which indicates that it is not just you being insulted.

But let none of you suffer as a murderer

Peter is not referring to suffering that should result from actual acts of murder, theft, or meddling. He continues to discuss our response to suffering in the name of Christ and explains something very important that we must not do. In verses 15 and 16, he distinguishes suffering as a Christian and otherwise. Although our suffering may be due to our association with Christ, Peter warns us not to endure it in the wrong manner. He then quickly commends the proper manner by which the saints should endure suffering and offers great encouragement to the saints.

Peter is not making a request, a suggestion, or stating a personal preference in verse 15. His statement is imperative. There are such things as those listed that Christians must not engage in, either by action or thought, when they respond to suffering in Christ's name. The list begins with murder and ends with meddling. It is a list that orders the egregiousness of the act from greatest to least but which all must be avoided. It becomes clear when contrasted with verse 16 that suffering for committing these acts and for being identified with them is not suffering as a Christian. Therefore, those who respond to suffering in this manner cannot be assured of all the blessing, rejoicing, and glory that Peter has been comforting the saints with for their suffering as Christians.

We may properly ask why these particular sins were listed, and others were not. Why were, for example, sexual immorality and idolatry not listed? Peter's deeper purpose becomes clearer as we continue to search the text for relevance to the context of the chapter. We might ask, does Peter think he is writing to murderers, thieves, and other evildoers who need to be reminded not to be so? He is writing to people who are or will be persecuted for their faith and made to suffer. Not everyone will follow his previous instructions to rejoice and bless those who harm them. Some may harbor thoughts of retaliation and revenge. That may lead to the sins of murder, theft, and other evil actions against those who cause the suffering and loss, if only by thought and desire.

During the Sermon on the Mount, Jesus explained that embracing the thought or desire for a sin bears the same guilt as the sin itself (Matt. 5:27-28). This is at the heart of Peter's purpose. It is as if he had written, do not harbor murderous desires in your hearts for those who cause you to suffer, for then you will suffer even as a murderer, or do not meddle in someone's affairs out of anger or retaliation to harm them for then you will suffer as a meddler. It is these sins of the heart that Peter is addressing that can be related to retaliation or retribution. Now, as he has called us to rejoice when we suffer for our association with Christ, committing sins of the heart against those who cause our suffering makes our suffering that of a sinner. It is a call for all saints to examine and guard their hearts when others make us suffer so that as we suffer, it is as a Christian, verse 16.

Yet, if anyone suffers as a Christian

In contrast to verse 15, Peter refers to suffering as a Christian. In his previous verse, this indicates that he explained how one suffers in a way that is not like a Christian and must be avoided. There is no shame in suffering as a Christian. He knows, as do we all from personal experience, that the labels thrust upon us by our adversaries are meant to shame us and cause us harm. From Peter's previous instructions, we may know that the Christian response to suffering is to rejoice (1 Pet. 1:6, 4:13) and bless those who do evil things to us (1 Pet. 3.9).

Instead of being shamed into silence, or worse, into a bad attitude, Peter exhorts us to glorify God, specifically for being named with Christ and a Christian. When we suffer for righteousness' sake, we will be blessed. We should not fear those who make us suffer or be troubled by it (1 Pet. 3:14). The saints have many good reasons to endure suffering for the right reasons and in the proper manner so that they can rejoice in being Christian and glorify God.

4:17-19 Suffering Part 2 "Judgment from a Faithful Creator"

Section 1 Pet. 4:17-19 is a continuation of 1 Pet. 4:13-16. These two sections need to be studied as one. Previously, Peter discussed suffering as a necessary part of God's eternal plan and encouraged us to endure and how to respond to it. Though we may not understand the reason for suffering, he has told us that there is a reason for it and that God will guard us through it, our faith being an instrumental factor. In verse 4:12, he expresses an expectation of more suffering yet to come upon the saints. He delineated the Christian response to this suffering in verse 4:16 in contrast with a non-Christian response in verse 4:15. Now, verses 4:17-19 are meant to instill the fear of God in us. And if we read them rightly, they do indeed.

1 Peter 4:17

For it is time for judgment

When we think of judgment in a Biblical sense, our minds turn to the last day when Christ appears, and the reprobates are cast into hell. As for the church today, it would be beneficial to recall the experience of the Israelites during Old Testament times.

The Old Testament history of the nation of Israel is that of a people being disciplined and judged by God. At that time, God's chosen people were known and seen as the nation of Israel. While it is proper to say that it is still Israel, the household of God is now known and seen as the church. The church is that body or household of God that receives his discipline because he loves the saints (Heb. 12:6). Certainly, God has not ceased disciplining his own household. In explaining 1 Peter 4:17, John Calvin explains the judgment Peter mentions as the ongoing chastisement of the church.

The specific Greek word from which *"judgment"* is taken in verse 17 is κρίμα (krima), which is translated elsewhere as *"condemnation."* biblehub.com defines this word as the result of judgment—damnation for the reprobate and eternal benefit for the redeemed. Certainly, God is chastising those he loves within the church and is not, in the same manner, chastising the ungodly, but is it Peter's intention to bring that before us?

In Romans 8:1, Paul writes, *"There is therefore now no condemnation for those who are in Christ Jesus"* (ESV). In that verse, condemnation is translated from κατάκριμα (katakrima). biblehub.com defines this word as the exact sentence handed down after due process and establishing guilt. The kata prefix indicates this is a verdict handed down. Otherwise, it is the same word as in 1 Peter 4:17. Romans 8:1 is about a verdict handed down following due process, a verdict of NOT GUILTY. So Paul can then say there is no condemnation. 1 Pet. 4:17 is about a judgment that has yet to occur. Both Paul and Peter are correct, and there is no contradiction. The saints must stand for judgment, but their verdict has already been determined.

Returning to verse 4:17, Peter has not written about ongoing discipline but judgment and has not written that it has begun within the church, only that it is time for it to begin. It is as if to say that the line has formed; we all stand in it and are ready to be judged. The logic of the verse does not allow us to think of chastisement only, for if the time has only recently begun for this to take place within the church, why was God chastising the Old Testament Church if the time hadn't begun for it then?

If it begins with us

As was previously explained, Christ is ready to judge the world. He was as ready in Peter's day as in ours, and we should be ready today to meet this judgment (1 Pet. 4:5). When judgment begins, it will begin with us, the church, the household of God.

Why does Peter bring judgment up here when he is writing about suffering for being associated with Christ (1 Pet. 4:14) and our response to that suffering? The response of anyone who is made to suffer because of their association with Christ will be taken as a reflection on Christ himself. Peter wants us to understand that this is a serious matter that fully deserves serious contemplation.

We begin in verse 17 by noting the word *"us"* in the phrase, *"if it [judgment] begins with us."* In context, Peter refers to the saints currently in the visible church. Judgment is about to begin with them, and we should note that not all members are saints. Who then is he referring to in the next phrase, *"who do not obey the Gospel of God."* They include all who have exchanged the knowledge of God for a lie, both outside and inside the church, regardless of their pretense of faith. That would include some who are among us but not of us. Thus, we are again forced to examine our hearts and guard them against all unrighteousness, even as we suffer. We should reflect on verse 4:15 and see in those words of the apostle that God is disciplining his people to strengthen them in times of trouble so that they will guard their hearts, for it is nothing less than judgment that awaits those whose profession of faith is nothing more than a pretense.

Matthew records a parable of Jesus that will help us understand that unbelievers in the church are ultimately weeded out. These concepts are precisely what Peter is drawing our minds to in verses 4:17-19 as both warnings and encouragements. Recall in the parable that a man sowed good seeds in a field. An enemy came in and sowed weeds among the wheat. They are allowed to grow together, but at the harvest, the reapers will gather the weeds to be burned, then gather the wheat into the barn (Matt. 13:24-30). Jesus explained that the Son of Man sows good seeds, which are the sons of the kingdom. The weeds are the sons of the evil one. The harvest is the end of the age when angels gather all causes of sin and law-breakers to throw them into the fiery furnace. Then the righteous will shine like the sun in the kingdom of their Father (Matt. 13:36-43).

Peter has not introduced something new. He has restated what he previously brought to light earlier in this chapter. The saints have these expectations. First, the suffering of the saints will end when Christ appears to judge the world. Second, the ones who have inflicted their suffering will go to perdition. But here we are dealing with ample reason for careful self-examination as we are drawn to contemplate our own judgment.

1 Peter 4:18

If the righteous is scarcely saved

We must remember that Peter is writing primarily to warn the saints of the profound necessity to guard our hearts so that, in the sight of God, we are found to faithfully be doing good, even as we suffer.

Peter poses a question that is meant to force us to contemplate our relationship with God and examine the nature of our assurance. Verse 4:18 begins with the proposition that a righteous person is only scarcely saved. He is not proposing that God's power to save is all but exhausted when saving a righteous person. Jesus touched on this subject during his encounter with the rich young man, as recorded in Mark. The disciples were very concerned after hearing Jesus say a camel can go through the eye of a needle easier than a rich man can enter the kingdom of God. Who then can be saved, they asked. Jesus responded that it is impossible for man, but all things are possible with God (Mark 10:25-27).

Peter is not leading us to contemplate God's power but our righteousness. What righteousness do we possess? If any, it begins with the external righteousness of Christ that was imputed to us. Progressive sanctification imparts actual righteousness that, in and of itself, is insufficient for us to approach God during this life. We are justified by Christ's righteousness, not our own. Peter intends to make us realize that even though we may be assured of being among the elect, it remains only in Christ that we may be counted among them, not for our glory but for his.

If anyone thinks they are good enough on their own to enter heaven, let them consider Matthew 5:48. "Good enough" falls far short of "*You therefore must be perfect, as your heavenly Father is perfect*" (ESV). The word being translated as *perfect* may better be rendered as *complete*. The only way a sinner can become a saint in the complete sense, as the verse indicates, is by the transforming power of Jesus Christ, which isn't applied until the rapture just before the perfected church is presented to the Father.

What will become of the ungodly and the sinner?

Then Peter brings the ungodly and sinner before us as if to ask what difference do you have from them? Initially, there is no distinction among men who have all sinned and are all sinners (Rom. 3:22-23). But there are spiritual differences as one lives according to the flesh and the other according to the Spirit (Rom. 8:5). Still, such difference is only by God's grace that regenerates, justifies, and sanctifies (Rom. 3:24). Thus the answer to Peter's implied question is that grace alone is the difference.

This is a brief diversion as we consider the whole of Romans 3:21-26 because it is an important passage that bears upon our study. These verses state that the righteous are justified by God's grace. That's how they become righteous. This grace is a gift. In other words, nothing has to be done by those it is given to. It is not earned or merited. From verse 3:21, God's righteousness is manifested through faith in Jesus Christ by all who believe.

Carefully note that the gift of righteousness that the righteous manifest by faith and belief in Jesus Christ is the righteousness of God. This gift is not given to all people but is given or withheld without distinction of person because all have sinned (Rom. 3:9, 22-23). Verse 25 goes on to state that this gift is received by faith. If you take this to mean that you are not justified and righteous until you have faith, like a gift you have to open, as some say, you've created a distinction and contradicted everything that Paul previously wrote. The correct meaning is that faith makes God's righteousness manifest (Rom. 3:21-22). When given the gift of God's righteousness, an elect saint is righteous in the sight of God immediately, but until he exhibits faith and believes, the righteousness of God that he possesses is not manifested. What does he believe other than believing in Jesus Christ and his righteousness before God? What came first, a person's faith that leads to righteousness or God's righteousness manifested by faith? According to this Romans passage, righteousness by grace comes first and is then manifested by faith.

Salvation vs damnation is a binary outcome. It is either one or the other without levels of distinction between these two extremes. And the only determining factor is the grace of God according to his purpose and will. Peter asks us to contemplate the outcome of the ungodly and sinner's life and what awaits them when judgment is rendered. In so doing, he brings us in our mind's eye to a precipice overlooking hell to examine the torments of the ungodly. Through this exercise of contemplation, we are forced to examine ourselves before God. Who am I, how am I conducting myself, and where am I headed?

1 Peter 4:19

Therefore, let those who suffer according to God's will

There are two levels to what this verse means. Superficially, we are reminded that all suffering is by God's will. Peter is not suggesting that suffering can occur outside of God's will. More significantly, he wants us to consider how we respond to suffering. Is our response according to God's will? When our response to suffering is according to God's will, we can entrust our souls to our faithful Creator. We can trust our souls through this life and the judgment to come to God because we are doing good now according to God's revealed will.

Since it does not take much to cause us to descend into ourselves and rely on our own strengths and means for a better outcome, Peter is directing us to entrust all that we are, our eternal souls, to what God's will is for us, even when we suffer and contemplate judgment. When we trust God to this extent, our conduct will be good.

Peter attaches a reason for this trust that God is a faithful Creator. By naming God Creator, he directs our thoughts to God's power to create out of nothing all things, his sovereign rule over what he has created, his ownership of creation, and his transcendence over creation. Peter applies the logic that if the greater is true, so must the lesser be true. Since God possesses the power to create all things and is sovereign over all things, he has the power and sovereignty to accomplish his will towards us. In addition to being Creator, God is faithful. He is faithful to his creation in that he can be trusted to accomplish all that he has said he will accomplish on behalf of his creation.

We may turn to the author of Hebrews to see what Peter means by the faithfulness of God. God promised in the covenant of grace that he would be the God of the faithful and that they would be his children. Then, he swore an oath to be faithful to the heirs of that promise. By his promise and oath, the heirs of the promise may be strongly encouraged and secure in their hope (Heb. 6:17-18). The oath God swore before Abraham is quite stunning. Abraham was instructed to gather several specific animals, cut them up, and lay their pieces along the ground in two rows. The Lord passed through these pieces as an oath to keep his promise to Abraham (Gen. 15:9-17). The significance of this oath is that should God fail to keep his promise, he would cease being God. That is quite impossible, and there was nothing subjective about this oath.

The faithfulness of God is an attribute, among others, that is proclaimed in association with his name. God has declared his faithfulness through the prophets. After smashing the original tablets of the law (Exo. 32:19), Moses was commanded to cut two new tablets and bring them to the Lord (Exo. 34:1). Here is what the Lord spoke to Moses.

The Lord passed before him and proclaimed, "The *Lord, the Lord, a God merciful and gracious, slow to anger, and abounding in steadfast love and faithfulness, keeping steadfast love for thousands, forgiving iniquity and transgression and sin, but who will by no means clear the guilty, visiting the iniquity of the fathers on the children and the children's children, to the third and the fourth generation*" (Exodus 34:6-7 ESV).

God's faithfulness cuts two ways. For the one, "*keeping steadfast love for thousands, forgiving iniquity and transgression and sin,*" but for the other, "*will by no means clear the guilty.*" He declares his faithfulness and righteousness together when promising to save his people (Zec. 8:7-8). The psalmists frequently praise God for his faithfulness and for being merciful, gracious, slow to anger, and abounding in steadfast love (Ps. 86:15).

As we can see, God is faithful in love to the elect, but he is also faithful in righteousness and will, as he has declared, "*by no means clear the guilty.*" In verse 4:15, Peter warns, "*But let none of you suffer as a murderer or a thief or an evildoer or as a meddler.*" And he asked us in verse 4:17, "*what will be the outcome for those who do not obey the gospel of God?*"

Now we come to verse 4:19, in which Peter brings to our attention the faithfulness of God, which is not only toward the elect to save but also to the reprobate to punish. Thus, Peter adds the caveat to our trust in the Lord "*while doing good.*" God is faithful to all his promises, those that promise salvation and deliverance and those that promise judgment and condemnation.

God has promised that he will guard the saints during times of suffering and that their suffering is a necessary part of his plan. Since Paul reminds us of God's faithfulness to his promises, it will afford us great assurance when we suffer, knowing that we will be delivered because God has promised. The ultimate deliverance is being saved.

Chapter 4 Summary

We are reminded of the life and its manner of sin that has been left behind since coming to Christ. Now, we live before God, who judges all people and calls us by his name to live holy lives of love and kindness to all and use our gifts to build up the church. All things are for the glory of God. Even as we experience trials and difficult times, we are called to regard Christ and his suffering so that we may rejoice when he appears. So now, as we suffer according to the will of God, we rejoice, knowing that we may entrust our souls to a faithful Creator. A memorable passage in chapter 4:

> As each has received a gift, use it to serve one another as good stewards of God's varied grace: (1 Peter 4:10 ESV).

Chapter 5 – Shepherding God's People

Introduction

Peter has been pursuing the theme of suffering. During the first five verses of Chapter 5, he seems to have departed from that theme to take up the subject of the church's government. However, we should view these first five verses through the lens of a suffering church. Shepherds of God's people who serve and honor Christ are always a blessing but are needed most when the saints face various trials.

Following these verses, Peter explicitly returns to the theme of suffering. Then, the epistle is concluded with final comments.

Peter draws our attention to Christ's appearing again in glory as he has previously in the following verses:

1:7- "at the revelation of Jesus Christ," which occurs on the last day,

1:13-"at the revelation of Jesus Christ,"

2:12- "glorify God on the day of visitation,"

4:7- "The end of all things is at hand,"

4:13- "when his glory is revealed," and

4:17- "For it is time for judgment to begin at the household of God."

Each instant has been to instruct and encourage the saints when tested, enduring trials and suffering, to draw our minds to the glory that awaits when Christ is revealed. He doesn't depart from this in Chapter 5. Peter writes:

5:1- "the glory that is going to be revealed,"

5:4- "when the chief Shepherd appears," and

5:6- "the proper time" refers to the time when Christ appears.

As we proceed through Chapter 5, we should keep the theme at the forefront of our minds and contemplate the reappearing of Christ in all of Peter's exhortations and encouragements to endure.

Peter's two epistles present a preeminently monergistic soteriology that God's grace is the sole source of the entire complex of salvation according to his will and power. 1 Peter 5:10 is extensively examined as an important example of Peter's soteriology.

5:1-5 Church Government

Peter must cover an important topic as he writes to a suffering church experiencing many trials and tests. He has already written of Christ's response to suffering as our example to emulate when we suffer. He has also addressed Christ as the Good Shepherd and our submission to authority, as God appoints all authority. He directly addresses those who hold authority within the church and how that authority should be conducted. The immediate recipients of his epistle were likely living in difficult circumstances from unkind, unfriendly, hostile, and dangerous people. They needed local shepherds to guide them faithfully through these difficult times and emulate Christ. We all need encouragement to hold fast with steadfast faith to that hope to which we have been called, and our shepherds play a critical role when they serve faithfully in difficult times.

The word translated as *elder* is the Greek word πρεσβύτερος (presbyteros). Paul explains to Timothy what the qualifications are but uses the term *overseer* from the Greek ἐπίσκοπον (episkopon) rather than elder (1 Tim. 3:1-7). When Paul gives instructions to Titus, he is told to appoint elders (presbyterous) in the local churches (Titus 1:5). In the same letter, Paul lists their qualifications and calls them overseers (episkopois) (Titus 1:7). We see then that elders and overseers occupy the same office whose primary duty is to shepherd the church in the name of Jesus Christ and for his glory.

Peter will spend a full chapter in his second epistle about false teachers, presenting their nature, conduct, and intentions, including their judgment and destruction. It is a chapter all teachers should read and heed, whether they are teachers within the church or the pagan world, especially those who strive to shipwreck people's faith. Please do not consider this an unimportant topic since, in our time, many churches have departed from the Biblical faith and the gospel of Jesus Christ while maintaining the labels and trappings of Christianity with which they present a false witness to the watching world. Biblical eldership is of paramount importance.

1 Peter 5:1

I exhort the elders

Different translations begin this verse differently. The ESV begins with "*So I exhort the elders...,*" the NASB begins with "*Therefore, I urge elders...,*" and the KJV begins with "*Elders who are among you I exhort....*" Peter is addressing the elders with an appeal, but what is not clear is whether or not this appeal is connected to what he has stated in previous verses, particularly in verses 4:12-19. Referring to the interlinear Greek text is not helpful since there are two sets of manuscripts. The ESV and NASB are based on the text that translates as "*Elders therefore among you....*" The KJV is based on the text that translates as "*Elders [the] among you....*" We are forced to make a decision. Is Peter departing from explaining the Christian response to suffering addressed in 4:12-19 and taking up a new subject, or is his appeal to elders connected to and related to instructions about suffering? I suggest the connection is real and a valid basis by which the opening verses of Chapter 5 may be understood in their proper context. Furthermore, following verse 5:5, Peter most clearly continues with instructions related to Christian suffering. In this sense, verses 5:1-5 do not comprise a departure from the theme of suffering, though they may appear to be so at the first reading.

Peter begins to address the local church elders by opening with, "*So I exhort the elders....*" Let us keep the "*So*" in its place and take notice that it connects verse 5:1 to what just preceded it. What follows is a consequence of what he has just written, or is at the least justified by it and should be considered in that context.

"*I exhort*" is attention-getting for what is to follow, which is of great importance that it should not be passed over lightly but deeply studied and taken to heart. Though Peter is an apostle, he sets that title aside to demonstrate to the elders he addresses that they have a great and grave responsibility, not unlike his own. He immediately refers to having witnessed the sufferings of Christ to secure in their minds that, nevertheless, he has the authority to exhort even the elders of a church and to impress upon them the importance of things to follow. He does not take the time to rehearse the sufferings of Christ, presuming they are known and understood by the elders.

Continuing to lay the foundation for his exhortation, Peter explains that he is a partaker of the future glory. Here, he presumes the glory is understood as he has identified it as that which is to be revealed. It is the glory of the sons of God when, at Christ's appearance, the united and perfected church is revealed. His purpose is not to elicit praise for himself but to impress upon the elders that they are also partakers of this glory. Just as they are elders in common with him, so are they partakers of the same future glory.

Through Peter's statement, we see his perspective on apostleship. Rather than expressing a preeminence over the other apostles as is claimed by the Roman Catholic Church, he presents himself as a fellow elder. In so doing, he is not debasing his apostleship but instead establishing eldership within the church in its proper position of authority and reverence. Scripture explicitly states what the offices and qualifications are within the church (Eph. 4:11; 1 Cor. 12:28; 1 Tim. 3:1-7, Titus 1:5-9). An apostle must be a witness to Christ's resurrection and directly called by Christ to the office of apostle (Acts 1:22; 1 Cor. 12:28). No man is an apostle today, even if their church claims he is.

1 Peter 5:2

Shepherd the flock of God that is among you

This is the beginning of the exhortation. The office or calling of an elder is that of a shepherd. It is their first and primary function. Among their primary duties are protection, preservation, and guidance. The metaphor is employed again when Peter refers to the believers under their care as a flock. The owner of this flock is God, and this is clearly stated to avoid misunderstanding. Shepherds are hired hands who shepherd someone else's sheep. If we consider the local church a flock, we may conclude that God possesses many such flocks. Elders are primarily to shepherd that flock, which is their local church. This may also be a limitation on the reach or extent of their oversight.

Exercising oversight

Here, Peter identifies the role of an elder. He is to be like a shepherd exercising oversight on behalf of God for the sake of those under his care. Exercising oversight is a continuous activity, not only when it is easy and convenient. To serve as God would have you serve is to willingly and eagerly shepherd his flock. In contrast, some exercise oversight for personal gain or only when compelled into service, which Peter says is shameful.

Why is it important for Peter to exhort elders to be shepherds of God's flock? His address to elders is important and must always be accepted and followed. When would it ever not be? Never. There are times when men must be reminded of the basic principles by which they live and serve within the church. The work of an elder has many difficulties. When other trials, tests, and sufferings are added, men lose sight of their calling and duties and must be reminded to remain focused on Christ and the church rather than on themselves alone. It is difficult to shepherd people in distress when you are in distress yourself, and thus, you may not pay much attention to the church's needs. The church needs spiritual comfort, strength, and assurance that cannot be provided by elders who abandon their calling, take it lightly, or perform it begrudgingly during times of distress and persecution.

1 Peter 5:3

Not domineering over those in your charge

Give a man authority over others, even a little, and he will find or invent ways to abuse it. Peter warns against that. The metaphor of being a shepherd is not without substantial meaning. He did not use terms such as boss, commander, or lord. Being called a shepherd does not make or turn an elder into a boss, commander, or lord. Jesus instructed the apostles that the Gentile rulers lord it over people, but that is not how it should be among you. You are to be as servants (Matt. 20:25-26). As this applies to the greater office, it does to the lesser office.

Nevertheless, when elders become domineering, they may cause grave and lasting injury to members of their church and even to their entire congregation. Even those who are domineering, unwilling, or only serve for personal gain are nevertheless elders and shepherds of the church until God removes them from office. Peter offers us no cause to think of such men as anything other than elders and overseers, regardless of whatever shortcomings or failures they may have. (The Westminster Confession of Faith Larger Catechism Questions 129 to 132 outlines the duties and sins of such men.)

Peter immediately orients our minds to one of the very purposes of being a godly shepherd: to be an example to the congregation. What example does he refer us to but that which exemplifies the shepherding care and nurturing love of Christ? Again, he leaves us to understand his meaning without being explicit, using his usual style of brevity and use of concepts. How wonderfully Christ provides for his church when the saints may look upon their elders enduring similar tribulations and witness examples of how Christ dealt with his suffering.

When the chief Shepherd appears

Peter draws our minds to the reappearance of Christ and addresses it with certainty. It is an event that will happen for which there is no doubt. He leaves us to realize that Christ is the Chief Shepherd, for there can be none other. This is an instance when there is some importance in what is not written. Peter uses the expression *"having been revealed"* as it appears in the Greek interlinear, which we find translated as *"when... appears."* The apostles did not write about Christ's return. Neither in the ESV nor King James translations is it ever written that Christ will return. It is only written as his appearing as in Titus 2:13. There is a reason for the use of "appearing" rather than "returns" that can be explained. The following verses confirm the indwelling of the Holy Spirit.

John 14:17- "The Spirit of truth dwells with and in you."

John 15:26- "I will send you the Helper, the Spirit of truth, from the Father."

Romans 8:9- "The Spirit of God dwells in you, the Spirit of Christ."

1 Corinthians 3:16- "You are God's temple and God's Spirit dwells in you."

2 Timothy 1:14- "The Holy Spirit dwells within us."

Other verses also proclaim that the Spirit of Truth, the Helper, the Spirit of God, and the Holy Spirit are all the same

Spirit of Christ (Eph. 4:4) and dwells in all the saints (Eph. 4:6). Thus, we may conclude that by his Spirit, Christ has never left us. Even so, God is omnipresent and immanent and never needs to return.

Peter is accomplishing several things by referring to Christ as the Chief Shepherd. First, he denotes that the elders' shepherding role is akin to Christ's shepherding. There is solidarity in this office, whether conducted by church elders or Christ himself. Second, he gently reminds the elders that their roles and duties as shepherds are overseen by Christ and that their authority is derived from and remains subordinate to him.

The unfading crown of glory

Elders will not receive "*a*" crown but rather "*the*" crown, which signifies its unique and special importance and value to be sought and cherished. They are battered by devils and men, and without hope of reward and steadfast focus, they are apt to perform their duties halfheartedly and weakly. When Paul addresses Timothy about his duties as an elder, he draws Timothy's focus to the same reward, the crown of righteousness given by the Lord himself (2 Tim. 4:8). Likewise, Jesus, through John, addresses the elders of the church in Philadelphia warning them to hold fast so as not allow anyone to seize their crown (Rev. 3:11). Holding fast refers to keeping Christ's word with patient endurance (Rev. 3:10).

This crown is referred to as "crown of glory" (1 Pet. 5:4), "crown of righteousness" (2 Tim. 4:8), and "crown of life" (James 1:12; Rev. 2:10). Some of its most important aspects are that God promises it (James 1:12), it is kept ready in heaven (1 Pet. 1:4), it is given by Jesus Christ (1 Pet. 5:4), and is unfading (1 Pet. 5:4).

Peter or any of the apostles could have written this exhortation to elders in any context, and it would have been a valid and enduring exhortation. But placed here, in the context of the church under trials and tests, it is of critical importance that the elders of the churches in Galatia, and by extension everywhere, do not waiver from their calling during times of difficulty.

1 Peter 5:5

Likewise, you who are younger, be subject to the elders

The word "likewise" connects what follows to that which has preceded. It indicates that they have something in common. In this instance, it is to keep one's focus on Jesus Christ as the chief shepherd and the reward that is kept even now for us in heaven. Thus, the younger members have a duty: to be subject to the elders appointed over them as they are subject to Christ. They are to do this eagerly and wholeheartedly in the same manner that elders are called to serve. Thus, the church's government may proceed unimpeded when the shepherding rule of elders is not opposed.

Clothe yourselves

Peter intends this exhortation to apply to everyone and explicitly states so. He does not mean to address only the church's younger members but rather all the saints, elders, and non-elders alike. The exhortation is to take up humility as if it were a garment and place yourself into it without partiality towards anyone. Elders are to be clothed in humility and to be humble toward those they oversee. Our inclination is to resist being humble. Peter brings us to the contemplation of benediction and malediction inherent to the appeal of humility. Only the humble person receives the benediction of grace—unmerited favor. Should anyone think of themselves more highly than others, regardless of their office, God, who is impartial, will oppose them. They will not enjoy the elevated impression they have of themselves when God turns their pride into shame.

5:6-11 Christian Conduct

The apostles have a propensity for setting our gaze on the panorama of the miseries of this life just before elevating our contemplation to the glories of Christ and the riches of our eternal inheritance. First, we are reminded of being under the mighty hand of God. Peter's reference to the "hand of God" is his way of reminding us that we remain under God's discipline and care. Then, he discloses that the purpose of God's discipline and care is so that we may be exalted at the proper time. This is an amazing encouragement and impetus for us to live humbly.

Although God's plan is for us to be exalted, there is danger from the devil for those who are not watchful and sober-minded to recognize and resist his schemes. He will test your faith as he does all the saints. However, Peter leaves us with this infallible hope that God will establish you because, by his grace, you have been called to Christ.

1 Peter 5:6

Humble yourselves

Peter writes, "*Be humble...*" It is not an option to be humble. There is benediction if one humbles himself and malediction if one does not. This has been established in the previous verse, which Peter now pushes further by drawing our minds to the contemplation of God's mighty hand under which we stand. But in so doing, he directs our thoughts toward the grace of exaltation as a gentle shepherd leading us with a promise rather than a prod. Even so, we must wait for this exaltation that will come at its proper time, thus indicating that the present is the proper time for us to be humble and patiently wait for a time to come when we will be lifted up. We may also infer from this that those who do not humble themselves may find themselves under the hand of discipline or not the recipients of this exaltation.

Let's return to Peter's explanation that the humble will be exalted at the proper time. Since it is called the proper time, it is neither arbitrary nor uncertain. It is established in God's eternal plan and cannot be altered. And as Peter writes, it is God who exalts the humble. Now we come back to being under the mighty hand of God, for it is nothing less than the power of God, exercised by him on our behalf, according to his eternal plan that in the proper time, the humble man will be exalted. We may look a few verses ahead to 1 Peter 5:10 about this exaltation, in which we read, *"And after you have suffered a little while, the God of all grace, who has called you to his eternal glory in Christ, will himself restore, confirm, strengthen, and establish you"* (ESV). The exaltation is profound and extensive. We'll look deeply into verse 1 Peter 5:10 momentarily.

1 Peter 5:7

Casting all your anxieties on him

While called to be humble and endure trials and testing for a season of unspecified duration, we are not left to our own devices for support. Here, Peter gives us a remedy and comfort for the things that trouble us, casting them all on the Lord. He reminds us that the very reason we can do this is because the Lord cares about us. The very nature of our coming to him with our cares and worries manifests his caring for us. We should note that this privilege of casting our anxieties upon God is a comforting grace for humble saints.

As such, it is most appropriate that Peter tells us to "cast" our anxieties upon God and not simply to recite them. The act of casting involves putting off and becoming separated from our anxieties. We read this sense by which casting separates in such verses as *cast off the works of darkness* (Rom. 12:12), *cast them [angels who sinned] into hell* (2 Pet. 2:4), and *perfect love casts out fear* (1 John 4:18). Peter does not provide specific insights as to how the causes of our anxieties may be resolved. Still, we may be assured that God indeed receives what he has urged us to cast upon him as relief from the persistence of being anxious and worried.

1 Peter 5:8

Be sober-minded

Before getting into verse 8, it seems from verses 1 Peter 5:8-10 that Peter is concerned with people questioning or even recanting their faith to be relieved of their suffering. These verses are of great encouragement and assurance, for they inform us of the great benefits of remaining steadfast in the faith even though we suffer. What may seem interminable is but for a little while. He begins by informing us that our real adversary is the devil and how we may defeat him by faith. Knowing that our brothers throughout the world suffer in the same way as we do redirects our minds from ourselves to them and encourages us to endure with them. Peter then leads us to contemplate the eternal glory of Christ to which we have been called and his grace that will establish us. Through the grace given by God, these verses will stir up in us that faith by which we may overcome the thought that our suffering is all for nothing.

Should anyone be deterred from being humble by alleging that humility in response to persecution, trials, and suffering may embolden those against them to greater severity, Peter has called them and us to be sober-minded as he has done twice before (1 Pet. 1:13, 4:7). There is a similarity in the contextual significance of these three exhortations to be sober-minded.

1 Peter 1:13- "for our living hope and the grace that will be brought to us when Christ is revealed,"

1 Peter 4:7- "to live in the Spirit as God does and the end of all things is at hand,"

1 Peter 5:8- "exaltation and eternal glory in Christ."

All three passages connect sober-mindedness to the anticipation of the grace and glory of Christ when he appears. This engages us to evaluate the eternal consequences of our actions and how we think about our circumstances and the things done to us.

Be watchful

Here, being watchful is put forth as an attribute of being sober-minded. A person cannot properly be sober-minded if he is not first watchful, knows to be so, and knows what to watch for. The call to be watchful implies there are harmful things to look for. At first, we need to place a watch on ourselves to guard against pride and arrogance welling up from within and thus make due adjustments when humility wanes. However, Peter is focused on his principal warning. There is an enemy whose goal and desire is to devour us. Although he does not explicitly explain what he means by "someone to devour," we may understand that if it were possible, the devil would rob us of all that we possess in Christ. His target is, from his perspective, one of opportunity.

That is, it could be anyone and, more likely, someone who is not on the alert and watchful. He does not know where to search but prowls around like a stealthy beast on the prey. He is likened to a roaring, ravenous lion. Of the devil, the apostles have written:

Ephesians 4:27- he is an opportunist

Ephesians 6:11- he schemes

1 Timothy 3:7- he sets snares (also 2 Tim. 2:26)

Hebrews 2:14- he has the power of death

1 John 3:8- he has been sinning from the beginning

Revelation 12:9- he is the deceiver of the world, Satan

1 Peter 5:9

Resist him

With such an adversary, we might fearfully think we cannot defeat him. But Peter briefly says, *"Resist him."* James gives us the same instruction with a noteworthy attachment that Peter most surely refers to. Resist the devil, and he will flee from you (James 4:7). The devil does not flee in fear but rather to search for a more pliable soul to ruin. James informs us of what the devil will do when we resist him, whereas Paul tells us what is required to mount a proper resistance: put on the whole armor of God, praying at all times in the Spirit (Eph. 6:10-18). Here is a list of the pieces of this armor.

— the belt of truth

— the breastplate of righteousness

— the readiness given by the gospel of peace

— the shield of faith

— the helmet of salvation

— the sword of the Spirit (the word of God)

The armor of God is a metaphor. Paul describes each piece, describing its meaning and purpose. Equipped with the things this armor represents, the saints can stand fast and resist the devil.

Firm in your faith

True resistance is made possible by being firm in your faith. A mere pretense of faith or a wavering faith produces only an appearance and not the substance of true resistance, which the devil will see through and by no means flee. The power of a steadfast faith foils the schemes and snares of the devil and repels the devil himself. Previously, faith was examined more fully in the comments on 1 Peter 1:5.

The suffering of brothers throughout the world

Peter adds this as an encouragement for those who think their suffering is too great a burden. Your brothers, the whole brotherhood of believers throughout the world, are suffering in like manner as you. He points out that you are not unique in your suffering or capacity to resist through faith.

1 Peter 5:10

After you have suffered a little while

Peter plays the brief time of "a little while" against

eternity. There is suffering for a "little while," but eternal glory in Christ awaits. Although suffering for a little while may seem interminable, it will end as he refers to a time after or following this time of suffering. This certainly encourages all who feel they may succumb to the burdens of faith.

The God of all grace

Peter is writing to a church in the midst of suffering for the faith, a persecuted church. Persecution may sometimes be subtle yet severe and challenge a person's faith to the brink of despair. He reminds us that God alone is the provider of all grace. There is no real grace unless God gives it. The hope of any substitute is a false hope. Any alleged grace that claims a different source is false. We must be reminded of this when enduring difficult times so that we don't search for relief from our designs or the designs of others. It anchors our trust in God, for the sole source of genuine grace is emphasized as Peter refers to God as "the" God whom we recognize as the one who has called us to his eternal glory in Christ. There is a subtle argument embedded in these words that since by God's grace we were called in Christ, we can be confident that his grace will prevail over our suffering.

The God of all grace is in full control and uses all grace in bountiful ways to grant us sufficiency for the times we live in and the circumstances we face, no matter what they may be. Thus, it is incumbent upon us to acknowledge that the grace we receive is from God. This is why it is proper to call God the God of all grace, for he is the only source of genuine grace. What's more, there is no mediator of God's grace other than

Jesus Christ (1 Tim. 2:5; Heb. 9:5, 12:24), whom the Scriptures declare is *"full of grace and truth"* (John 1:14).

We properly think of grace as unmerited favor, but that favor comes with the power of Almighty God, who makes his grace abound to fulfill its purpose (2 Cor. 9:8, 12:9; Eph. 3:7). Thus, we can correctly say that the grace that God gives to people always fulfills its purpose irresistibly. It would be foolish of Peter to call our attention to the God of all grace, to encourage us if his grace could be of no avail.

God has called you to his eternal glory in Christ

There are two parts to this section of 1 Peter 5:10: (1) who has called you, and (2) to his eternal glory in Christ. If we discuss them separately, we will not fully apprehend what Peter is trying to impart. The phrase is compressed in its theological content and in the time spanned by what it refers to. Being called and coming to glory are separated by time, though he expresses them together. Indeed, they are together because the saints have been called to future glory. We will first deal with the theological content of the section.

The *who* in the passage is, of course, the Father, the God of all grace. The focus of 1 Peter 5:10 is the Father; it is patricentric, and thus, we are to contemplate the Father as we study it. Furthermore, the verse is theologically monergistic, meaning that God alone accomplishes the entire complex of salvation, whereas faith manifests the blessings received by grace alone. As to our calling, volumes can be written.

The proclamation of the gospel that goes out to the world is not the calling that Peter is writing of. That is the general calling to which people, dead in trespasses and sin, cannot respond favorably. Why? Simply because God is sovereign over who is predestined unto glory and who is not (Rom.9:10-13), he does not share or impart his sovereignty to individuals (Deu. 4:24). The saving power of God to release a soul bound in darkness lies in the Gospel (Rom. 1:16), in Jesus Christ (1 Cor. 1:24), and in the word of the cross (1 Cor. 1:18), not in human reason or will. God sovereignly exercises this power according to his will and purpose, not us. As scripture says, "*I will have mercy on whom I have mercy, and I will have compassion on whom I have compassion*" (Exo. 33:19; Rom. 9:15). Thus, the calling of which Peter is writing is that which is joined with God's mercy, compassion, grace, and power according to his sovereign will and purpose. As such, it irresistibly accomplishes its purpose so that the saints know they will come to God's eternal glory in due time, having been called to it.

The origin of this call is God's love with which he loved and chose us in Jesus Christ before the world was created (Eph. 1:4-5). Paul goes on in Ephesians to explain that the Father chose us to be holy and blameless and predestined us for adoption as sons, blessed us in the Beloved, redeemed us through Christ's blood, and graciously forgave our trespasses. (Eph. 1:5-7). What the Father did in all this was with all wisdom and insight and lavished it upon us (Eph. 1:8). In all this that Paul has explained, he has not come to our call until the next verse, *"making known to us the mystery of his will, according to his purpose, which he set forth in Christ"* (Eph. 1:9 ESV). All of what Paul has explained means nothing to us unless and until the Father makes it known because otherwise it is a veiled mystery (2 Cor. 4:3; Eph. 3:4; Col. 1:27, 2:2, 4:3). This is the Father drawing us to Christ (John 6:44), simply making known to us the mystery of his will.

By his grace alone, God's eternal and immutable power was invisibly at work from before creation to this day to bring us to Christ. Having our minds and hearts set this way on our gracious God and Father, we may have all assurance that the same love, grace, and power through Jesus Christ will complete the work he began in us (Phlm. 1:6). Paul also says that those whom the Father predestined he also called, and those whom he called he also justified, and those whom he justified he also glorified (Rom. 8:30). Being glorified is being brought to the eternal glory of the Father and Christ, and we see that Paul expresses with such certainty as to claim it is already accomplished. Indeed, all that is necessary for the elect to come to glory has been accomplished, and Peter wants us to rest our hope and security on that.

The glory Peter writes of in this section is the intrinsic glory of the Father. He repeats that we have been called to the Father's glory in 2 Peter 1:3. It is through Jesus we are brought to glory (John 6:44). He is indeed writing of the Father's glory but also of the elect being brought to it. We may wonder how this is possible in light of what God told Moses. When asked to see God's glory, Moses was warned that no man could see

God's face and live (Exo. 33:20). When the saints are caught up in the air to meet Christ when he descends from heaven (1 Thess. 4:17), they are changed to be in his image (Rom. 8:29), like him (1John 3:2). From that moment we will bear God's image in a way we have never before bore it and which no reprobate ever will. Then the saints, the perfected church (Matt. 5:48), holy and blameless (Eph. 1:4), without spot or blemish (2 Pet. 3:14), no longer in bodies of flesh but with spiritual bodies (1 Cor. 15:44), will come before the Father (2 Cor. 4:14; Eph 5:27; 1 Thess. 3:17; 2 Pet. 3:18). Thus, we come to the Father's eternal glory and rather than perishing, we become partakers of the divine nature (2 Pet. 1:4). In few words, Peter establishes the perseverance of the saints which was his intention for our comfort and assurance.

Peter could have just written that we are brought to the Father's glory, but he added that we are brought to his eternal glory. It is as unfading as his aseity. It incorporates all attributes of God that constitute his intrinsic glory. There can be no doubt among God's elect that no matter how long the church on earth must wait for the Lord to appear in the clouds with his mighty angels, God's glory will be just as magnificent as ever.

Now, we can deal with the practical content of the section. Peter addresses our need for comfort, assurance, and encouragement while experiencing difficult, faith-challenging times. He is not reciting the basic principles of the faith to new believers. He is drawing our minds to that which lies at the foundation of our faith and which we reasonably understand. He intends us to recall, reflect, and embrace it again. As Paul encouraged Timothy, let us also fan into flame the gift of God, recalling it is the spirit of power, love, and self-control (2 Tim. 1:6-7).

In Chapter 5, Peter refers to our calling so that we may think about our lives, how we live, and particularly our faith with sober minds. If we think of Chapter 1 as doctrinal, then Chapter 5 is application. Being humble, casting our anxieties on God, resisting the devil, and being firm in the faith are applications founded on the doctrines Peter draws to our attention, especially needful during times of suffering.

Likewise, Peter is not recapitulating or establishing the glory of God in Christ but is inviting us to reflect on it. The Greek texts vary as to the inclusion of the name Jesus. The ESV leaves it out, while the KJV includes it. He discloses the eternal nature of God's glory by which he enforces our knowledge of the eternal nature of our calling, that we have been called to eternal things and have been called to abide in God.

Will himself restore

Peter told the Galatians in verse 1 Peter 5:6 that there is a proper time when God will exalt them, and by extension, we may understand that this applies to all the saints in Christ. In verse 5:10, he expands on that exaltation. This happens at a time characterized as *"proper"* and is associated with our calling to God's eternal glory in Christ. To understand Peter's meaning, we must consider this expanded description of "exalt" in the light of Christ's appearance. Each of the terms, restore, confirm, strengthen, and establish, share similarities but with distinctions. Restore is probably better translated from the Greek as perfect, as in the culmination of our sanctification. What occurs when the saints meet Christ in the air at his reappearing should be contemplated.

The Greek word translated here as confirm is sometimes translated as strengthen and vice versa but relates to spiritual knowledge and power. With these two terms, Peter impresses upon us that our perfection will be fixed and will involve spiritual knowledge and power imparted to us (2 Pet. 1:3). To be established is to be grounded and settled. By the mighty hand of the God of all grace (1 Pet. 5:6, 10), the saints will be perfected, confirmed, and strengthened when Christ appears and thereby established in fulfillment of that to which they have been called. This is the proper time for the suffering of the saints to end and such a wonderful and blessed hope in the present time that we should embrace with all assurance that when Christ reappears, the saints will be established blameless in holiness from within by the Lord, and confirmed since this is *before* or in the sight of God (1 Thess. 3:13).

1 Peter 5:11

To him be the dominion

Unable to contain his praise, Peter breaks into a brief doxology of God's eternal power. The KJV renders this slightly differently, "*To him be glory and dominion for ever and ever.*

Amen." Peter also made the same statement of praise earlier in 1 Peter 4:1.

We must not conclude that Peter only ascribes sovereign authority and power to God since he previously included glory. As to God's glory, Peter has just written in the previous verse that we have been called to his eternal glory in Christ and has declared it to us. But here, we are to focus on God's sovereign authority and power since this is also meant for our encouragement. God can accomplish all he has promised because he has dominion over everything.

5:12-14 Closing Remarks

Peter commends Silvanus and Mark to the church so they may be well received. Silvanus is a faithful brother, and Mark is regarded as a son to Peter. Also, the saints at Babylon sent their greetings. These statements are helpful and needed to establish the faithfulness of people in a church beset with false teachers and devils.

Peter affirms this epistle is the true grace of God and that we should stand firmly in it. Everything he wrote in this epistle is the word of God, the source of all grace. Thus, he puts to rest all claims that openly speak against what he has written, and we may conclude that such claims have no grace in them and might be a scheme of the devil bent on leading the saints astray.

On the one hand, he recommends faithful people to the saints who can be trusted to speak the truth. On the other, he affirms the veracity of his epistle as the word of God to equip the saints against those who falsely present themselves as brothers, wolves in sheep's clothing (Matt. 7:5; Acts 20:29).

1 Peter 5:12

Silvanus

Silvanus is mentioned by name several times by Paul in his greetings (2 Cor. 1:19; 1 Thess. 1:1; 2 Thess. 1:1). He is also mentioned twelve times in Acts by the name Silas and is seen as a major participant with Paul and Timothy and a servant of the church.

Paul mentions Cephas [Peter] to the Corinthians in 1 Corinthians 1:2 and 3:22, indicating that the Corinthians know who Peter is. So, we might be able to place Peter and Silvanus together in Corinth, Greece. However, Peter likely knew Silvanus as a leading man among the brothers before this since the apostles (including Peter) sent Silvanus to Antioch with Paul and Barnabus (Acts 15:11). Peter and Silvanus knew each other very well, and Silvanus is likely Jewish. There are different opinions on Silvanus' role in Peter's letter. Did he assist Peter in writing the letter, delivering the letter, or both? It seems likely from the text that he assisted Peter in its writing.

I have written briefly to you

Peter acknowledges that his epistle is short, but although it is short, it exposits and conveys the true grace of God with exhortations and declarations. This is addressed to bring to nothing the schemes of those who oppose or doubt the grace of God and work to shipwreck people's faith. He encourages everyone in the faith to stand firm in the exhortations he has declared because the grace of God empowers them to that end. We will defeat the devil's schemes and not be led astray by standing firmly on the truths Peter has presented.

1 Peter 5:13

She who is at Babylon

There are two opposing views for the location Peter refers to as Babylon. The first is that he wrote from Rome and used the word Babylon to hide the church's identity in Rome from persecutors. In their commentaries on 1 Peter 5:13, Matthew Henry and John Calvin state that this is Babylon in Assyria since the diaspora of Jews was the largest there.

According to britannica.com, the strongest evidence that Peter was in Rome is in a letter to the church at Corinth by Clement of Rome (authorship is ascribed to Clement). Here is a quote from his letter to the Corinthians:

> "But not to dwell upon ancient examples, let us come to the most recent spiritual heroes. Let us take the noble examples furnished in our own generation. Through envy and jealousy, the greatest and most righteous pillars [of the church] have been persecuted and put to death. Let us set before our eyes the illustrious apostles. Peter, through unrighteous envy, endured not one or two, but numerous labours; and when he had at length suffered martyrdom, departed to the place of glory due to him" [https://www.newadvent.org/fathers/1010.htm].

There are two considerations regarding this evidence. The letter does not claim Peter was in Rome when he was martyred. Clement I, or Clement of Rome, is claimed to be the first pope and the third successor of Peter. Such a claim necessitates Peter to have been in Rome. This would be consistent with the Roman Catholic office of the pope, which is extra-biblical and man-made. The logic is circular and self-serving. Clement was in Rome, and he was claimed to be Peter's third successor since Peter was in Rome. These considerations do not dispute the possibility that Peter was ever in Rome; they just indicate that Clement's letter doesn't establish his presence there, as some claim.

Peter employs a metonymy to refer to the saints in the church at Babylon by referring to the church itself. According to him, the church has been chosen to indicate that the saints comprising that church are among God's chosen people. They have been chosen just as they have been the recipients of Peter's letter, and he makes this clear. It is both a confirmation and an encouragement.

The original text uses the phrase *"elect with [you]"* rather than chosen, συνεκλεκτὴ (syneklektē), (biblehub.com). Elect is a specific term with doctrinal significance leading to adoption through Jesus Christ. Furthermore, the churches, or more specifically, the saints within the churches, were elected with one another, not just in like manner. This signifies the church's unity, and that election itself is a single act of God that is not a work that is spread over time. Recall that in 1 Peter 1:1, Peter referred to his audience as "elect." In verse 1

Peter 5:13, the same basic word is used except that it is "elect with." The ESV could have rendered the translation closer to the original language.

Sends you greetings, and so does Mark, my son

The church at Babylon sent greetings to the many churches across Asia Minor. Peter includes this greeting to encourage and strengthen his audience. This was indeed the case and not just an amenity for him. So, in all likelihood, the saints at Babylon would have read his epistle before attaching their greeting to it.

It is held that Mark, mentioned here, is John Mark, the writer of the Gospel. There is no reason to doubt this. He is a cousin of Barnabas (Col. 4:10). Mark was with Paul during his Roman imprisonment when Paul wrote Colossians and with Peter when Peter wrote 1 Peter. It is too uncertain when these letters were written to place Mark with Peter and Paul in Rome simultaneously. Peter knew of Mark's family, his mother, and perhaps Mark himself while in Jerusalem. After being released from prison by an angel, Peter went to Mark's mother's house, as recorded in Acts. A group of believers were meeting there. When Peter came to the house, he knocked on the door. A servant girl recognized his voice, which indicated her familiarity with him and his having visited there before. He didn't stay but departed, indicating that he had gone there to console the group by telling them how he came to be freed by an angel rather than to seek security. His visit also indicates his familiarity with the group and concern for them (Acts 12:12-17).

It's not clear when the two became associates, but it is clear from Paul that Mark had matured as a Christian man of faith and had become a great help to Paul, as he has to Peter. The spiritual dimension of being someone's son indicates that Peter had much to do with Mark's faith and maturity. Peter takes possession of Mark's growth by calling him "my son" rather than "a son," establishing Mark's reputation as a faithful, trustworthy servant of God to the church.

1 Peter 5:14

Greet one another with a kiss of love

Verse 5:14 begins with an exhortation to abide in loving affection for one another. One must actively engage another to greet them with a kiss of love, and this forestalls all inclinations to the contrary. Do not avoid the one who has upset or harmed you somehow, but go to them and express affection in the manner of your approach. We are creatures who endeavor to build walls between ourselves and those who hurt or disappointed us. While Peter does not address that directly, the implications of verse 5:14 forbid that.

Verse 5:14 is a benediction on two counts. First in sequence is the blessing of being loved by fellow saints, followed by peace for all who are in Christ. As for peace with the Father, the saints, by being in Christ, have peace with the Father (Rom. 5:1; 1 John 4:10).

In the opening greetings of most epistles, the writer expresses peace for their readers who are in Christ. This can be found in:

Romans 1:7	1 Timothy 1:2
2 Corinthians 1:2	2 Timothy 1:2
Galatians 1:3	Philemon 1:3
Ephesians 1:2	2 Peter 1:2
Philippians 1:2	2 John 1:3
Colossians 1:2	Jude 1:2
1 Thessalonians 1:1	

Likewise, peace is also expressed for the saints in several benedictions (e.g., 2 Cor. 13:11). As in other benedictions and greetings, Peter is not expressing a desire for the peace of propitiation, which already exists by being in Christ, but the peace that should exist among the saints as an outflowing of mutual affection. The apostles John and Paul wrote about this peace, in

John 16:33- "I have said these things to you, that in me you may have peace,"

John 14:27- "Peace I leave with you; my peace I give to you. Not as the world gives do I give to you,"

John 20:19- "Jesus came and stood among them and said to them, "Peace be with you,"

John 20:21- "Jesus said to them again, "Peace be with you,"

Rom. 12:18- "If possible, so far as it depends on you, live peaceably with all,"

Rom. 14:17- "For the kingdom of God is not a matter of

eating and drinking but of righteousness and peace and joy in the Holy Spirit,"

Rom. 14:19- "So then let us pursue what makes for peace and for mutual upbuilding."

As we pursue Peter's intention concerning peace, we see this is consistent with the nature of God. God is routinely called "God of peace."

Rom. 15:33- "May the God of peace be with you all. Amen,"

Rom. 16:20- "The God of peace will soon crush Satan under your feet,"

Phil. 4:9- "practice these things, and the God of peace will be with you,"

1 Thess. 5:23- "Now may the God of peace himself sanctify you completely,"

Heb. 13:20- "now may the God of peace who brought again from the dead our Lord Jesus."

We are called to seek peace among the saints in many places.

1 Per. 3:11- "let him turn away from evil and do good; let him seek peace and pursue it,"

Heb. 12:14- "Strive for peace with everyone,"

1 Thess. 5:13- "Be at peace among yourselves,"

Rom. 14:19- "So then let us pursue what makes for peace and for mutual upbuilding,"

2 Pet. 3:14~ "be diligent to be found by him without spot or blemish, and at peace,"

Mark 9:50~ "Have salt in yourselves, and be at peace with one another."

So, we conclude that God presents himself to us as the God of peace who desires that we be people of peace ourselves, striving to be at peace with one another. Peter's benediction is that we receive, partake, and enjoy this peace among the saints as a blessing of being in Christ. This is consistent with the opening phrase of verse 5:14, which exhorts us to show loving affection toward each other, inherent among people at peace with one another.

We might ask, why does Peter confine this benediction of peace to those in Christ? Being at peace with the world, in the same way as with the saints, is dangerous. Paul tells us directly not to have any fellowship with the lawless deeds of darkness by being unequally yoked with unbelievers (2 Cor. 6:14). Yes, we are to be at peace with unbelievers as much as is possible for us. Still, Paul warns us to do so at a safe distance. 2 Corinthians 6:14 has far-reaching implications that church leaders should pay closer attention to, given the state of cultural intrusions into the church. Peter's second epistle addresses false teachers and people who scoff at the truth.

Chapter 5 Summary

Peter addresses a church suffering persecution and nearing the end of the apostolic age. What will become of the church when the apostles can no longer provide sound guidance and discipline? The gospel must be taught and defended faithfully by men called to shepherd Christ's church on his behalf, particularly to this small fledgling church. They are called and appointed by Christ and given authority to be used on behalf of the church and not for personal gains. The flock is enjoined to submit to their shepherds, who are examples of Christ, particularly as they share in his suffering and exemplify his response.

The overarching theme is that of enduring while suffering. We are called to be humble, submissive, and sober-minded. We are called to be watchful, that is, to know our circumstances and conduct and to resist the devil so that he will flee from us. We are always to look with great expectation for the coming of the Lord on the day of judgment so that our minds and hopes are set on God's promised glory, an assurance that will guide our every day. By such, Peter lays out the godly conduct of a suffering church that will persevere to the day of the Lord. The chapter and epistle close with a doxology and benediction.

Memorable passages from Chapter 5 are:

Casting all your anxieties on him, because he cares for you.
(1 Pet. 5:7 ESV)

Be sober-minded; be watchful. Your adversary the devil prowls around like a roaring lion, seeking someone to devour. (1 Pet. 5:8 ESV)

And after you have suffered a little while, the God of all grace, who has called you to his eternal glory in Christ, will himself restore, confirm, strengthen, and establish you. (1 Pet. 5:10 ESV)

THE END

About the Author

Following his service as a pilot in the Air Force, Dr. Dayton earned his PhD in physics from the University of Connecticut. While in the Air Force, John became a Christian and has since served the church as a deacon and elder. Shortly after beginning graduate school, he got married; he and his wife of 45 years have two adult children and four granddaughters. Now that John has retired from his tenured professorship at a private college, he has turned his efforts to writing expository commentaries on books of the Bible.